COSMO SERIES SOVIET UNION
Copyright by
RAND McNALLY & COMPANY
Made in U. S. A.

SOVIET POTENTIALS

A Geographic Appraisal

SOVIET POTENTIALS

A Geographic Appraisal

George B. Cressey

MAXWELL PROFESSOR OF GEOGRAPHY
SYRACUSE UNIVERSITY

SYRACUSE UNIVERSITY PRESS

1962

Library of Congress Catalog Card: 62:8478

COPYRIGHT © 1962 BY SYRACUSE UNIVERSITY PRESS

MANUFACTURED IN THE UNITED STATES OF AMERICA

CONTENTS

v

LIST OF MAPS

LIST OF TABLES

INTRODUCTION

The Theme

Does the Union of Soviet Socialist Republics have the environmental potentials with which to become the world's greatest state? This volume provides a brief appraisal of material assets and limitations as seen by a geographer.

This book is built around three ideas which relate to the strength of nations. The first concerns the continentality of the Soviet Union, not merely in terms of remoteness from the climatic influence of the ocean but also in its isolation from the stimulus of world commerce and international ideas. The second theme deals with the environmental handicaps of poor terrain, short growing seasons, and limited rainfall, which place restrictions on normal agriculture. The third idea emphasizes the Union's vast mineral resources, among the richest in the world, which give the promise of great industrial and political strength.

In any analysis of Soviet geography, people are the most significant component, always outweighing the environment, and *Soviet Potentials* attempts to evaluate why they live where they do.

Within a few decades, the Soviet Union has emerged from an undeveloped agrarian country to become a major industrial power. Some areas are congested and well developed, others almost empty and untouched; it is therefore wise to look at the map in regional terms. Geography cannot evaluate all of the potentials but it can inventory the assets and limitations, and locate the areas of major promise or difficulty.

Soviet resources appear to be a mixture of very good and rather poor; what man does with them is another matter. The Union has indeed set an audacious goal, no less than that of surpassing the United States; what does geography have to say as to this possibility?

The Background

Soviet Potentials is the outgrowth of three earlier volumes: *How Strong Is Russia?* (Syracuse University Press, 1954), *Asia's Lands and Peoples* (McGraw-Hill, second edition 1951), and *The Basis of Soviet Strength* (Whittlesey House, 1945), each of which finds echoes in these pages by permission of the publishers.

This book is also based on four trips to the Soviet Union: 1923, 1937, 1944, and 1960. These travels have extended from the Baltic to Lake Baikal and from the Siberian Arctic to Middle Asia, and have included five trips across the Trans-Siberian Railway.

Since 1935 the author has taught courses on Soviet geography, and many of the ideas here presented are the outgrowth of class discussions and dissertation research. Each scholar stands on the shoulders of his predecessors, and so each book has scores of authors.

This volume would not have been possible without assistance from many sources, notably aid from Syracuse University, a Hill Foundation lectureship at St. Olaf College, work with the Editorial Board of the Great Soviet World Atlas, field work made possible by the Northern Sea Route Administration, excursions in connection with the International Geological Congress and the International Congress of Orientalists, and grants-in-aid from several foundations and councils.

Communist Economic Objectives

The Twenty-second Congress of the Communist Party of the Soviet Union, meeting in 1961, adopted an elaborate program aimed at the transition from socialism to communism. This voluminous document provides a broad historical review and sets audacious tasks. The following fragmentary paragraphs are quoted, without comment, in order to set Soviet goals against the geographic potentials as discussed in the remainder of this volume.

In the current decade (1961–1970), the Soviet Union . . . will surpass the strongest and richest capitalist country, the U.S.A., in production per head of population; the people's standard of living and their cultural and technical standards will improve substantially; everyone will live in easy circumstances; all collective and state farms will become highly productive and profitable enterprises; the demand of the Soviet people for well-appointed housing will, in the main, be satisfied; hard physical work will disappear; the U.S.S.R. will become the country with the shortest working day.

In the next decade (1971–1980) the material and technical basis of communism will be created and there will be an abundance of material and cultural benefits for the whole population.

. . . With these aims in view, the C.P.S.U. plans the following increases in total industrial output:

Within the current ten years, by approximately 150 per cent, exceeding the contemporary level of U.S. industrial output.

Within twenty years, by not less than 500 per cent, leaving the present over-all volume of U.S. industrial output far behind.

. . . Electrification, which is the backbone of the economy of Communist society, plays a key role in the development of all economic branches. . . .

. . . The annual output of electricity must be brought up to 900,000–1,000,000 million kilowatt-hours by the end of the first decade, and to 2,700,000–3,000,000 million kwh. by the end of the second decade. . . . A single power grid for the whole U.S.S.R. will be built. . . .

. . . The further rapid expansion of the output of metals and fuels, the basis of modern industry, remains one of the major economic tasks. Within twenty years metallurgy will develop sufficiently to produce about 250,000,000 tons of steel a year. . . . A steady effort will be made to insure priority output of oil and gas. . . .

. . . The growth of the national economy will call for the accelerated development of all transport facilities. . . .

. . . A single deep-water system will link the main inland waterways of the European part of the U.S.S.R. . . .

The following must be achieved within the next twenty years: in Siberia and Kazakhstan—the creation of new large power bases using deposits of cheap coal or the waterpower resources of the Angara and Yenisei Rivers . . . in areas along the Volga, in the Urals, North Caucasus and Central Asia—the rapid development of the power, oil, gas and chemical industries and the development of ore deposits. The Soviet people will be able to carry out daring plans to change the courses of some northern rivers and regulate their discharge for the purpose of utilizing vast quantities of water for the irrigation of arid areas.

. . . Along with a powerful industry, a flourishing, versatile and highly productive agriculture is an imperative condition for the building of communism. . . .

. . . In order fully to satisfy the requirements of the entire population and of the national economy in agricultural produce, the task is to increase the aggregate volume of agricultural production in ten years by about 150 per cent, and in twenty years of 250 per cent. . . . In the first decade the Soviet Union will outstrip the United States in output of the key agricultural products per head of population. . . .

. . . To insure high, stable, steadily increasing harvests, to deliver agriculture from the baneful effects of the elements, especially droughts, to steeply raise land fertility, and to rapidly advance livestock breeding, it is necessary: . . . to improve soil fertility, to carry through a far-flung irrigation program, to irrigate and water millions of hectares of land in the arid areas and improve existing irrigated farming, to expand field-protective afforestation, building of water reservoirs, irrigation of pastures and melioration of over-moist land, and to combat, systematically, the water and wind erosion of soil. . . .

Soviet Geography

Whenever Soviet geographers are asked to define their subject, the usual reply is, "The function of geography is to develop the productive resources of the State." As with most Soviet science, there is little room for cultural aspects; geography must be practical. Soviet geography also aims to change the environment so that man may alter the areal organization of productive forces. This is reflected in the large number of geographers employed in every planning board, both of the central government and of the individual republics, and in the many geographic field surveys which precede planning.

With the planned control of the national economy, and with the integrated use of resources over wide areas, there is a large demand for geographers who have competence in branches of the field. Soviet geography thus penetrates into many contiguous sciences. As examples, for regional and city planning, geographers are employed who are well trained in economic geography and in geomorphology; for land evaluation, geographers are trained in soil science, physical geography, cartography, and economic geography; for the rational management of forestry, geographers are trained in botanical geography, hydrology, and economic geography; and for planning water-economy systems and waterways, geographers must be qualified in hydrology, climatology, and economic geography.

In the schools and universities of the Soviet Union, the principal focus of geography is on the links between natural phenomena, population, and economy in different countries and regions of the world, and on the regional study of nature and productive forces in the U.S.S.R. Professional geographers are trained in 30 out of 40 universities. In addition, 60 Teachers' Institutes, out of 200, prepare teachers of geography. In addition to these university centers, there are Institutes of Geography under the several Academies of Science, both Union and Republic.

GEORGE B. CRESSEY

Syracuse, New York
January, 1962

SOVIET POTENTIALS

A Geographic Appraisal

Chapter I

ONE-SEVENTH OF THE EARTH

In all the world there is no other country quite like the Soviet Union. Here is one of the most striking social and political developments of our times. Regardless of whether one favors or opposes communist ideology, the Union of Soviet Socialist Republics challenges our attention.

Many factors combine to fashion a nation's geographic potentials; some physical, some human; some static, some dynamic. Nature has contributed a distinctive environment, but the resources were present in czarist days; what has happened since 1917 is a tribute to the Soviet people.

Within a few decades the Soviet Union has become a major world power. This is partly the product of a dynamic idea, but it is also a measure of the environmental possibilities. Is this indeed a great nation with a bright future, or is it merely a spectacular one with limited potentials?

No one can travel across the Soviet Union without being impressed by the material resources of the country and the industrial accomplishments of Soviet planning. It is clear that the Union has developed a tremendous capacity to do things in a big way. At the same time, the

Much of the culture of old Russia centers around the Red Square outside the walls of the Kremlin. The mausoleum of Lenin appears in the foreground, with the cathedral of St. Basil at the end of the Square; beyond it flows the Moscow River. The new Moscow is symbolized by the skyscraper apartment in the background. (*Courtesy U.S.S.R. National Committee, I.G.U., Moscow*)

Union faces impressive environmental limitations. Mountains, drought, cold, infertile soils, and poor accessibility characterize vast areas, and limit the agricultural potentials.

The Soviet Realm

The prospects of the Soviet Union are to be measured in terms of its land and its people. This is by far the world's largest state; it ranks third in population after China and India. It is also the most diverse; within its boundaries lies a wide array of environments. Here is room for all of the United States including Alaska, plus all of Canada, plus Mexico. Within the eight and one-half million square miles of the Union there is space for the whole of North America. Here lies one-seventh of all the land on earth, one-twentieth of the entire globe.

Continentality is thus the key word in Soviet geography. While the Union of Soviet Socialist Republics borders the ocean on three sides, most of it lies deep within Eurasia. No other great nation is so land-locked, or has such seasonal extremes of climate, or is so remote from the ideas which cross the high seas.

Continental size proved to be an advantage during both world wars, for there was room into which the government might retreat, buying time by selling space. Defense in depth is impossible in a country the size of Belgium or Poland; these small countries lasted only a few days, while large nations such as the Soviet Union, even though hard-pressed, could retreat and take advantage of their great area.

What is not so obvious, but of basic importance, is that most of this vast country lies in the latitudes of Canada rather than of the United States. The great water bodies of the southern Soviet Union, such as the Black, Caspian, and Aral seas, lie on a parallel with the Great Lakes of North America: Superior, Michigan, and Erie. Those parts of the Union which resemble the United States correspond to Montana, the Dakotas, and Nevada. Much of the Soviet Union is like the land around Hudson Bay. Nowhere does Russia have a Mississippi Valley; nowhere is there an Iowa or an Ohio. Here is an Asiatic replica of Canada rather than of the United States. Only small parts of the Soviet earth are really good. Much of their best farmland is inferior to that of Minnesota.

If a map of America were to be superimposed on Eurasia, it would be seen that the boundary between Montana and Saskatchewan bisects the Ukraine. Kiev matches Winnipeg, and Odessa on the Black Sea lies in the latitude of Duluth. Where the Soviet Union reaches farthest south into the deserts of Middle Asia, conditions resemble those of

Novosibirsk is the metropolis of Western Siberia. This railway station lies 2,000 miles east of Moscow, but is only one-third of the way to the Pacific. (*Courtesy U.S.S.R. National Committee, I.G.U.*)

Nevada, with Alma Ata in a setting similar to that of Salt Lake City. The northernmost settlements in Siberia are less than a thousand miles from the North Pole. Leningrad's west coast position is comparable to that of Skagway, Alaska, and the east coast port of Vladivostok is on the parallel of Halifax.

One important difference between the continents of Asia and North America lies in the mountain pattern. The Soviet Union has no Sierra

---

Natural Vegetation and Cultivated Land (*map on following pages*)

Four major vegetation zones cross the Soviet Union. Two of them are lands of cold: the tundra and the forest; two are lands of drought: the steppe and the desert. Each zone has its gradations according to moisture and the length of the growing season. Coniferous softwood forests, known as the taiga, dominate the north, with deciduous hardwoods in the west and center. Mountains interrupt the zonal regularity and introduce local patterns according to elevation and exposure.

Agricultural land occupies an irregular area, for the most part carved out of the mixed forest and grassland zones, widest in the west and tapering eastward toward Lake Baikal. Each dot represents 5,000 hectares (approx. 12,500 acres). Data from *Great Soviet World Atlas,* adjusted for 1960 conditions.

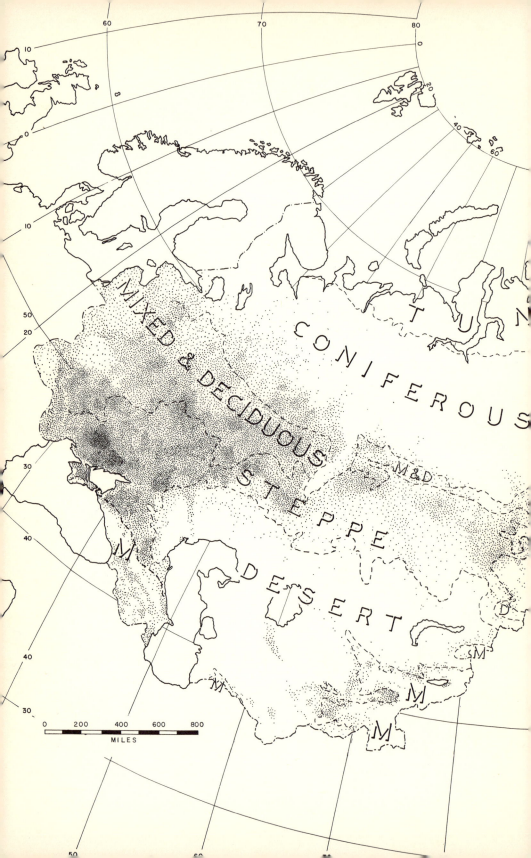

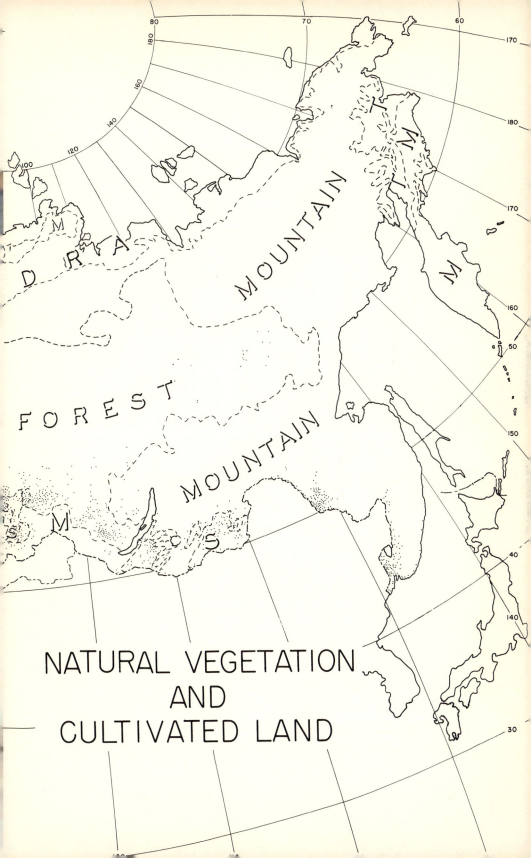

NATURAL VEGETATION
AND
CULTIVATED LAND

Reindeer are widely used in the tundra lands near the Arctic Ocean. Native peoples catch fish along the rivers and coast in the summer, and trap for furs in the interior during winter months. (*Tass*)

Nevada or Cascade Mountains on the west to keep out moisture from the ocean, although Scandinavia and Switzerland form partial barriers. On the other hand, high mountains along the south of the Union block moisture from the Indian Ocean, in contrast to Canada's supply of rain from the Gulf of Mexico. Asia is much larger than either of the Americas, and the seasonal contrasts between summer and winter are more marked. Whereas North America covers a great range from north to south, the Soviet Union extends from west to east. This means a somewhat more uniform climate in the U.S.S.R., with no humid tropics.

Like the United States, the Union faces two oceans. Since contacts with the open Atlantic and the Pacific are restricted, they are more like those of Canada than the United States, but they do give the Soviet Union an outlook to both the east and west. There is a long frontage on the Arctic, but this has only limited value. If the country should want to develop a large international trade, the ocean outlets are poor and the many land frontiers are blocked by deserts and mountains.

Only toward central Europe is there level land for easy rail connection. An examination of the globe makes it clear that the Union is poorly located for world leadership; the country lies in the least accessible part of Europe and the most isolated part of Asia.

Poor accessibility is as basic in Soviet geography as continentality and high latitude. Vast areas are remote from railways, roads, or navigable rivers. The Soviet Union has some eighty thousand miles of railways, as compared with three times that mileage in the much smaller United States. While there is a closely spaced network in the west, large sections elsewhere are far from rail lines.

To appreciate distances within the U.S.S.R., measurement should be made in time as well as in miles. Every day at five o'clock the Trans-Siberian Express starts eastward from Moscow. Nine days later the train reaches Vladivostok. Attached to the train when it leaves Moscow are cars which originated at the Polish frontier, 6,284 miles from the Pacific. This is by far the longest train trip on earth. The distance is equal to that from San Francisco to London, for the Soviet

Forests cover three million square miles of Soviet territory, some of it excellent timber. This view is in the taiga near Lake Baikal. (*Tass*)

Union covers the full width of the United States plus the entire span of the Atlantic Ocean. Within the U.S.S.R. are eleven time zones, or 171 degrees of longitude.

Trans-Siberian Railroad
Express Timetable

Day	Kilometer	Hour	Station	River
1	0	17:00	Moscow	Moscow
1	360	23:44	Yaroslavl	Volga
2	454	1:35	Buy	
			(Junction from Leningrad)	
2	962	10:56	Kirov	Vyatka
2	1442	20:33	Perm	Kama
3	1822	4:54	Sverdlovsk	
3	2146	11:27	Tyumen	(Tobol)
3	2719	23:11	Omsk	Irtysh
4	3345	10:50	Novosibirsk	Ob
4	3574	16:11	Taiga (Junction for Tomsk)	
5	4107	3:14	Krasnoyarsk	Yenisei
6	5196	4:50	Irkutsk	Angara
6	5685	16:03	Ulan Ude	Selenga
			(Junction for Mongolia)	
7	6243	5:40	Chita	Ingoda
8	7911	0:28	Kuibyshevka	
			(Junction for Blagoveschensk)	
8	8568	17:53	Khabarovsk	Amur
9	9337	13:45	Vladivostok	Pacific Ocean

All hours shown are Moscow time
Elapsed time Moscow-Vladivostok Express: 212¾ hours
   Ordinary through trains: 254¾ hours
Above hours are arrival time (except Moscow); add 20 minutes for departure time.
Add 799 km. and 14 hours for Moscow-Minsk-Polish Frontier

To travel from north to south by rail may be even more difficult than to cross from the Atlantic to the Pacific. Only two railways reach the Arctic Coast: the line to Murmansk and that to Salekhard near the mouth of the Ob. The southernmost railway in Middle Asia extends to the Afghan border, 2,200 airline miles to the south. To make the trip by train would require extensive detours, several changes of cars, and a week of travel. No such north-south rail journey is possible across Siberia.

Much of the country's traditional inaccessibility has been altered by the airplane, for jet services span the continent in a few hours. All major centers are linked with Moscow, though in many cases not directly with each other.

Where rail or air services are unavailable, travel is slow, for Soviet roads are poor and boat service infrequent.

Landscape Patterns

The basic pattern of the Soviet landscape is easily described. Four broad vegetation zones—tundra, taiga, steppe, and desert—cross northern Eurasia from the Atlantic almost to the Pacific. Mountains interrupt the continuity, and there are local modifications, but this fourfold pattern sets the stage for land use. The map of natural vegetation provides the key to rainfall, seasonal temperatures, drainage, soil, and topography, and thus to potential crops and population densities. Of all environmental maps, this is the most meaningful.

Next to the Arctic lies a belt of treeless tundra, inhospitable and uninhabited. South of the tundra is a great evergreen forest, the world's largest. This is known to the Russians as the taiga. Short summers and acid soils make agriculture unattractive. The tundra and the taiga are lands of cold; to the south of them are two lands of drought: the steppe and the desert. The steppe has a cover of short grass, while the desert is nearly barren. Only as one travels from north to south do these contrasts appear; from east to west across the Union there is essential uniformity. A trip on the Trans-Siberian Railway for the most part follows the boundary between the forest and the grassland, and so fails to give a picture of the north-to-south contrasts.

Agriculture occupies a fifth or middle zone, carved out of the taiga and the steppe. Half the cultivated land is cleared forest, half is plowed grassland. The soils and climate of this area somewhat resemble those of the northern Great Plains of the United States and the Canadian Prairies.

The tundra is a rigorous landscape which offers little to man. Some of it is completely lifeless and barren; in more favored areas one may

---

RAILWAYS (map on following pages)

The map of Soviet railways reflects the pattern of population and of agriculture. The central parts of Soviet Europe are well served with a closely spaced rail net, so that most areas are within a few tens of miles from a railway. In Middle Asia the net is coarser, and large areas are more than 100 miles from rail service. Northern Siberia is without railways, so that many settlements are 1,000 miles from the Trans-Siberian.

Since cross-country automobile roads are undeveloped and navigable rivers are widely spaced, poor accessibility characterizes two-thirds of the Union.

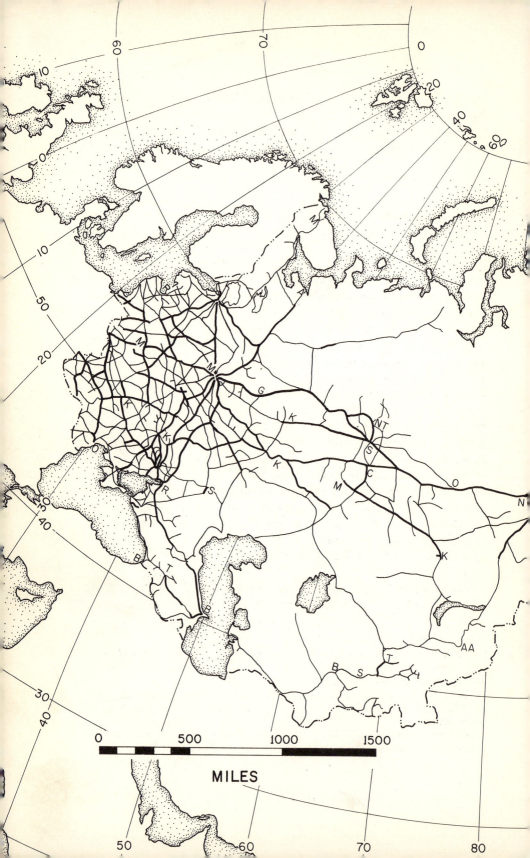

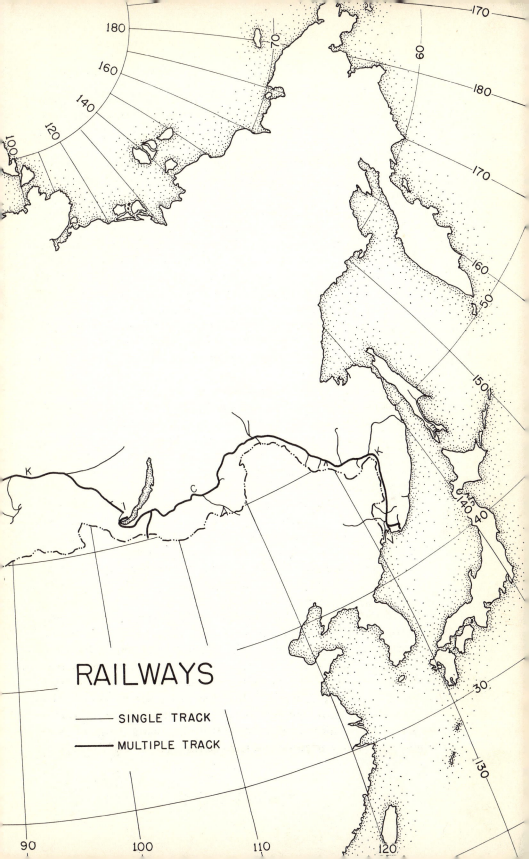

RAILWAYS

—— SINGLE TRACK

——— MULTIPLE TRACK

find stunted trees and dwarfed bushes. Mosses, lichens, and low
shrubs are the normal vegetation. Similar conditions prevail in northernmost Canada and Alaska. At these high latitudes, winters are as
dark as they are long. July days may have continuous sunshine, but
the sun is so low that it never shines warmly. Cultivation is impossible,
for "summer" lasts barely a month or two, and frost occurs during ten
or eleven months each year.

The tundra borders the ocean for thousands of miles, but the sea is
frozen much of the year and is of limited economic or climatic value.
Navigation is gradually being extended through the Arctic Ocean, but
the possibilities are unattractive. The only resources for livelihood in
the tundra are the fish of the streams and the sea, and the fur-bearing
animals of the interior. During the brief period when rivers and lakes
are not frozen, man becomes a fisherman; during the winter, he traps
for furs. Snowfall is generally light, but it remains on the ground
throughout the winter. The reindeer live on mosses and lichens, and
when the snow crusts over they cannot break through to find their
food, so that many may die.

Travel across the tundra is by reindeer or dog sled. Outside the few
settlements, most of the scanty population perforce lives a nomadic
life. Their total number is low, and life is hard, for this inhospitable
land offers small attraction for settlement. Many of the people are
non-Russians, an assortment of nationalities akin to American Eskimos.
Next to Finland there are the Lapps, and farther east the native people
include the Evenki and Chuckchee.

Here and there, Arctic mineral resources have led to the development of a mining community. This is the case around the Khibin
Mountain in the Kola Peninsula, where vast deposits of apatite supply
the basis for phosphate fertilizers. Coal, copper, and oil are also found
here and there beneath the tundra. These widely scattered mining areas
have brought numerous settlers, but their impress on the total tundra
landscape is insignificant.

South of the tundra, in a broad belt from the Atlantic to the Pacific,
lies a great coniferous woodland. This is the taiga, the world's largest
forest, with an area of some three million square miles, one-fifth of the
world's forest land. The Soviet taiga is similar in character to that
which crosses Canada. Next to the tundra, near the Arctic Circle, trees
grow slowly and are stunted, so that the forest has no commercial
value. Larch may grow but two inches in diameter in a century. This
area is even more empty of population than the tundra. Large areas in
the north are nearly impassable due to fallen trees, a tangle of bushes

and vines, and swamps. This is no place to make a forced landing while flying, for even if one can walk away from a wrecked plane, there is no place to go. There are few roads, and travel is on sleds, by boat, or through the air.

Farther south, warmed by longer summers, the stunted Arctic taiga gives way to excellent forests of pine, spruce, and larch. In normal years, large shipments of lumber move to Western Europe, but so great is the current domestic need that there is little surplus for export. The Soviet Union is in the midst of a boom economy and the demand for lumber is heavy. Despite extensive cutting, the normal growth is so vast that the country can look forward to timber supplies for a long period; conservation is for the future. Wood is still the cheapest fuel in many areas.

Forty per cent of Soviet forests is made up of larch; pine covers 16 per cent of the area, birch 13 per cent, and spruce 11 per cent, while cedar and fir account for 5 and 3 per cent, respectively. Oak is the leading hardwood but occupies only 1 per cent of the forest area.

The original forest cover has largely been cleared from the now-cultivated agricultural plains in Soviet Europe, but excellent stands of commercial timber remain in the hill lands of the Urals and elsewhere. The Soviet Union as a whole is deficient in hardwoods such as oak and maple, so that most furniture, railroad ties, and log houses must be made of less durable softwoods.

While the greatest forest areas of the Union lie in Siberia, lumbering operations have developed chiefly in areas more accessible to the market needs of the western areas. East of Leningrad are two large lakes, not much smaller than the Great Lakes of North America, and around their rocky shores are coniferous forests. The timber of this area enabled czarist St. Petersburg to become one of the major lumber ports of Europe.

The decades since the revolution of 1917 have seen a great increase in the construction of housing, especially in the cities. Expanding industry and railroads have also called for large amounts of lumber. Trees are usually rafted to sawmills, so that every river carries its quota of logs. The junction of a river and a railroad in the taiga is sure to signify the presence of a sawmill.

Because of the abundant supply of wood, log houses are the rule in farms and villages throughout the taiga area. Sawed lumber for homes is used only in the cities. Each Russian log house has its huge wood-burning brick stove, and these often occupy a quarter of the kitchen. Taiga winters are cold, and in many areas the house foundations are banked with moss or sawdust, while over the log ceiling there may be a foot of earth to provide insulation.

Most of these log houses are drab and stereotyped, entirely without decoration or personality. Paint seems to be almost unknown. In each village, however, there are usually a few more elaborate log houses, former homes of the now-liquidated kulaks. These houses have ornate decorations around the roof, fancy metal work on the chimneys, and once had painted shutters. Since winters are severe, double windows are common. In the spring, the space between these windows serves as a greenhouse, for most Russians are very fond of flowers.

Even old city houses with brick construction for the first floor may have logs for their second story. This may be for economic reasons, but perhaps it also reflects the peasant background of so many Russian people. The Soviet Union is rapidly becoming urbanized, but it will be some time before the new factory workers forget their farm background.

The Russian village in the cleared forest area is a random collection of log houses, in most cases strung along a single street for a mile or more. Behind each house is a shed or barn for the farmer's cow and chickens. These are his personal property, but the bulk of his income comes from his share in the collective farm. Rising above the larger villages is an old Russian Orthodox church, with its characteristic rounded domes. Most village church buildings are now used for what the government terms "socially useful purposes," although churches still function as such in the larger cities.

The sweep of communist socialism has profoundly affected economic life, yet social conditions change slowly. Inside many simple farm houses one may see traditional ikons—and in some there are still old, much repaired, but still serviceable Singer sewing machines.

Natural grasslands occupy large areas south of the forest. This is the steppe, an area of short grass, unlike the tall lush grasslands of the Illinois prairie but similar to the dry lands of Montana and Saskatchewan. Most of the area is flat to rolling, and in years when the rainfall exceeds 15 inches, this is an attractive area for the farmer. Unfortunately, rainfall in the steppe often drops to half this amount, so that tragic famines have been recurrent. At such times, great numbers of people in the Ukraine have starved and millions have died. In areas where the average rainfall amounts to 10 inches or less, conditions become too precarious for agriculture, and even grazing is uncertain. These dry steppes are the traditional home of the Cossack horsemen.

Steppe lands extend eastward from the Black Sea area of the Ukraine to the Pacific, passing through Mongolia and Manchuria. Only the northern half of the steppe is cultivated; the south is too dry. At times when the rainfall is above normal, or when the light snowfall melts slowly and sinks into the ground, excellent crops are possible. In other years, crop yields are unpredictable. Parts of the Soviet steppe resemble the American "dust bowl." When the cover of vegetation is removed, erosion by wind and water follows. To check this erosion and in an attempt to ameliorate the climate, extensive shelterbelts have been planted. Trees will grow in the steppe if planted in humid years and watered while young so that their roots may reach into the moist subsoil, but they seldom reproduce themselves.

Since forests are lacking, the houses are built of sod. Blocks of turf are piled up for walls, with openings for doors and windows. Roofs are flat, made of logs and covered with earth. The rainfall is so low that a foot of earth on the roof is usually adequate. Vegetables may even be grown on the roof. Since the steppe has cold winters, double windows are the rule.

Agriculture in czarist Russia was characterized by long narrow fields.

Semi-arid grasslands spread from the Ukraine far eastward into Siberia. These horses belong to a collective farm in the dry steppe near Kuibyshev. (*Sovfoto*)

This strip cropping resulted from the successive subdivision of farms through inheritance, and was often inefficient. Fields half a mile in length might be only a hundred yards wide. Only traces of this old practice remain, for private farming is extinct.

Under the Soviets, farms have been collectivized, or are operated by the State. Even from the air, one can tell when he crosses from the capitalist world into communist territory by the changed appearance of the farm landscape. Small peasant plots have been made into large farms. Fields are merged and tractors largely replace the horse-drawn plow. Giant farms are especially noteworthy in the broad steppe lands of the lower Volga. Wheat is the dominant crop in the steppe, with rye as a more tolerant crop in the cooler areas. Grain elevators dot the landscape of the grasslands. Whereas old Russia was a large exporter of wheat, domestic demand now leaves little surplus. When the Soviets do ship wheat, it is usually for political reasons.

The expanding population in Russia calls for more food. Some of this increased need has been provided by improved seeds, some by a more efficient use of existing cropland, and some through the cultivation of new land, either through dry-farming techniques or through irrigation. Not much more unused good land remains, so that agricultural pioneer-

Much of Soviet Middle Asia is arid, a product of its remoteness from the ocean and the descending air masses. These sand dunes are in the Turkmenian Republic. (*Tass*)

ing is coming to an end. While there may be some increase in farmland through clearing the forest, the major prospects lie in the steppe, especially where rivers such as the Volga may supply irrigation water.

Beneath the steppe lands lies an exceptionally rich black soil, high in organic matter and with unleached mineral plant nutrients. This is known to the Russians as chernozem. If the chernozem only had more rainfall, harvests would be large. But, unfortunately, if the rainfall were heavier, these particular soils would not have developed. Chernozem soils lie in a west-to-east belt from the Ukraine into Siberia.

Farther north, in the forest, chernozems are replaced by acidic podsol soils. These are less suited to grain production, but are so extensive that they form the mainstay of Soviet agriculture. Podsols are developed under a coniferous forest, and are of only moderate fertility. Many of the podsol areas are poorly drained. Two other soils reflect the pattern of climate and vegetation; the tundra soils of the Arctic, and the desert soils of the arid south.

Much of Soviet Middle Asia is a desert, or at least a semi-desert. Rainfall is but 5 to 10 inches, for the area is remote from the ocean. Even in the south, winter temperatures are below freezing, and summer temperatures rise well above 100° F. This dry land continues from the Caspian Sea eastward across Mongolia into China. Parts of it are a sandy waste; elsewhere a scanty vegetation makes it possible to graze sheep or cattle. Near the mountains of Soviet Middle Asia, rainfall is slightly higher and ground water comes closer to the surface so that some dry farming is possible. Irrigation possibilities are limited to the vicinity of the streams, especially those which rise in the snow-covered mountains along the southern frontiers of the U.S.S.R.

Throughout this arid zone, as in most dry lands, man is traditionally a nomad, taking his flocks to the grass since the latter is too short to be harvested and stored in barns. This is the home of many non-Slavic peoples, the Kazakhs, Uzbeks, and Turkmens. Each nationality has its picturesque dress and customs; only within the past century have these peoples come under Russian control.

Successive tides of conquest have swept across these deserts, leaving monuments to rulers like Tamerlane, who built Samarkand with its blue tiled mosques and tombs. From the deserts of Central Asia came the Golden Horde of Mongols who overran much of ancient Russia.

Within the lowland areas of these four major landscape zones of tundra, taiga, steppe, and desert live most of the Soviet Union's people. Two other unique environments need to be added: subtropical areas near the Black Sea, and the high mountains of the south.

Crimean coastal landscapes owe their subtropical character to the warming influence of the Black Sea and the near-by mountains which block cold air masses from
the north. (*Courtesy U.S.S.R. National Committee, I.G.U.*)

The southern shore of the Crimea is a Soviet Riviera, sheltered from
polar winds in winter by low mountains parallel to the Black Sea and
tempered in summer by the adjacent sea. Here grow grapes and or-
anges, and early vegetables supply the metropolitan markets farther
north. Palm trees attest to the mild climate.

The Crimea is the traditional vacationland of the Russians. During
the days of the czars, many nobles built villas here in order to enjoy
the subtropical advantages of both summer and winter along the Black
Sea. Today, these residences provide rest homes for favored Soviet
workers. Many factories own hostels in the Crimea where employees
who exceed their production quotas are rewarded by free vacations.
Here too is Yalta, where the famous wartime conference was held.

Somewhat similar conditions prevail south of the Caucasus Mountains at the eastern end of the Black Sea, near Sochi and Batumi. This
is an area of citrus crops and of rice fields cultivated by water buffalo.
The rainfall reaches 100 inches in one area, highest in the Soviet Union.

Whereas Russia once imported tea from China, this subtropical corner of the Caucasus is now a tea-growing region, with an annual production of several million pounds. Both the Crimean and Caucasian areas of mild climate are small in extent, and their classification as subtropical in a latitude more than 40 degrees from the equator is only marginal.

Alpine mountains border the U.S.S.R. all the way from the Black Sea to the shores of the Pacific Ocean, with zones of climate and vegetation according to their altitude and exposure. Unlike the nomads of the desert who move horizontally in their quest for grass, many mountain pastoralists move up and down the slopes with the seasons. These ranges reach their highest point in the Pamir Highlands where maximum elevations exceed four miles. From this core area, lower ranges extend west to the Caspian and through the Caucasus to the Black Sea, as well as east and north along the borders of China and Mongolia.

Permanent snow fields and long valley glaciers are found in many of the higher ranges from the Caucasus to Kamchatka. This is a glimpse of the Tien Shan in the Kirgiz Republic. (*Tass*)

Political Structure

The Union of Soviet Socialist Republics is a federal union of 15 separate republics, each representing a broad racial classification and each with a certain measure of internal autonomy. The highest administrative authority for the Union as a whole, under the guidance of the Communist Party, is the two-house Supreme Soviet, divided into the Soviet of the Union and the Soviet of Nationalities. Members of the former are elected by regional voting, with one deputy for each 300,000 people, irrespective of race. The Soviet of Nationalities is chosen according to nationality as represented by the several republics and their ethnic subdivisions.

Within most union republics are a series of subdivisions which reflect either nationality or economic considerations. These are variously known as autonomous republics or autonomous oblasts, both based on racial conditions; and krays, oblasts, okrugs, and rayons.

The entire U.S.S.R. covers 8,650,069 square miles, or 22,402,200 square kilometers, with a population during the 1959 census of 208,-826,650. Details may be found in the Statistical Tables at the end of the book.

By far the largest and most populous of the Union republics is the Russian Soviet Federated Socialist Republic. Here live over 120,000,000 people, and here are 6,500,000 square miles. Moscow is both the capital of the Union and the R.S.F.S.R. While the term Russia is often employed for the entire Union, this is an incorrect use of the word.

Next in population comes the Ukrainian Soviet Socialist Republic, with 40,000,000 people, and its capital at Kiev. Adjoining it is the Byelorussian or White Russian Republic. Along the western frontier are also the Estonian, Latvian, Lithuanian, and Moldavian republics. The former Karelo-Finnish S.S.R. has been absorbed into the Russian S.F.S.R.

Within the Caucasus region lie the Georgian, Azerbaidzhan, and Armenian republics. Five republics lie in Middle Asia: the Kazakh, Turkmenian, Uzbek, Tadzhik, and Kirgiz. The first of these, the Kazakh S.S.R., stands next to the Russian S.F.S.R. in size with an area of over a million square miles, about as large as the other 13 republics combined.

This political organization has evolved since 1917, with important territorial changes following the Second World War. It is well to recognize that the geographic extent of Russia has grown over the centuries. Much of the Caucasus was once under Persian control, while Middle Asia was formerly a series of separate kingdoms. China once claimed nearly a million square miles of what is now Siberia. Over the centuries, Russia has grown continuously; the only area once part of the country but now independent is Finland.

Rapid postwar urban growth characterizes most Soviet cities. This is a view of apartment houses along the main street of Kiev. (*Photo by Y. Berliner*)

Chapter II

POPULATION BACKGROUNDS

THE KEY to Soviet strength lies in the people—well over two hundred million of them. Only two nations of the world have a greater reserve of manpower, and in few other countries have people of such varied origins been welded together to build a strong nation. Many Soviet citizens have been captured by the thrill of developing a new country and of discovering the material wealth which lies within the Union of Soviet Socialist Republics. In this respect, Soviet pioneering achievements are not unlike those which characterized the United States after the Civil War.

Only four census enumerations have been made. In 1897, the total population was found to be 129,200,200, while in 1929 it was 146,980,-460. These figures are not comparable as to area, for after the revolution of 1917 the country lost parts of Finland, Poland, and areas along the other frontiers. There was also great loss of life during the First World War and the ensuing revolutionary years. The 1939 census total was 170,191,000. The census of 1959 gave a total of 208,826,650, and reflected a loss of several million people as a consequence of the Second World War. Data for the last two returns are given in the Statistical Tables, with the distribution between urban and rural inhabitants.

The faces of these Young Pioneers in the Soviet Arctic suggest the vitality and enthusiasm of Soviet youth. Nearly 200 "nationalities" live in the Soviet Union, many of them Turkic or Mongoloid in background. Slavs account for only three-quarters of the total population. (*Courtesy Northern Sea Route Administration, Igarka*)

The Emergence of Russia

The original home of the Slavic peoples appears to lie northeast of the Carpathians, from where they began to migrate in the first century. The present Bulgars and Serbs represent a southern group, the Poles and Czechs a northwestern division, while the eastern group is divided among the Great Russians, White Russians, and Little Russians or Ukrainians.

During the ninth and tenth centuries Slav settlements are mentioned as far north as Estonia, and as far east as the region between the Don and the Volga. Their earlier history is lost in the mists of uncertainty, and their western contingents, except in language, were not clearly differentiated from the Germanic tribes. Evidently all of them were comprised by the historian Tacitus in his *Germania*.

As a political unit, Russia did not come into existence until the ninth century. At that time there lived in the regions along the Dnieper and farther northward a group of Slavic tribes, not yet united. Their dissensions finally led to a proposal that they call in some prince of foreign blood, of whom none would be jealous, and under whom, in consequence, it might be possible to merge all the subdivisions into one strong state. Slav envoys thus called on certain princes of the Varangians, of Scandinavian origin. These were three brothers, the oldest of whom was called Rurik. They were offered the privilege of becoming the rulers of the tribes and, upon their acceptance, the Slav territories were divided among them. Shortly after, the two younger brothers died and the entire nation became united under Rurik.

In the opinion of some historians, however, the fact may have been that the Slavic tribes, suffering from repeated incursions of the much better armed and trained Scandinavians, hired other Varangians for their protection, and these ended by usurping the ruling power over the tribes. The term "Rus" appears at about the same time. It is probably derived from *rusij*, meaning fair-haired or blond, a general characteristic of the Slav people in these regions.

After the days of Rurik, the bulk of Russian history consisted of internal accommodations, often violent; of defensive or retaliatory external wars; of fluctuating life-and-death struggles in the south and southeast with the Asiatic hordes; and of unceasing extension of the prolific Slav element in all directions where resistance was not insurmountable. This expansion took place especially toward the northeast and northwest, where the primitive Finnic strains were replaced or absorbed.

Notwithstanding the many vicissitudes of the country, its spread continued until 1226, when all of southern Russia fell under the final Tatar or Mongol invasion. This invasion covered all of the present Ukraine and extended over much of Poland, Galacia, Hungary, and some of eastern Germany. The southern Russians were overwhelmed and subjected to Tatar yoke, or forced to flee. Large areas in the south and southwest became seriously depopulated and were occupied by the roaming Tatars of the Golden Horde. The cultural progress and the racial aspects of Russia were greatly affected by the Tatar invasion of the thirteenth century. The descendants of the Tatars are found to this day along the Volga and its southern tributaries, north of the Sea of Azov, in the Crimea, and in the Caucasus.

About the same time that the terms Ukraine or Little Russia came into vogue, there also began to appear those of Velikorussia or Greater Russia, and Byelorussia or White Russia. These names are partly conventional and partly environmental or geographical. The language and habits of the Byelorussians, who occupy the western part of the Soviet Union, were gradually affected by their relations with the Poles and Lithuanians. The Velikorussians or Muscovites, who had spread over the central, northern, and eastern regions, were modified in language and habits by their associations with the various people of Finno-Ugrian stock with whom they mingled and whom they freely absorbed.

Such is the origin and nature of the three large subdivisions of the Russian people. The differences between them, cultural, temperamental, and anthropological, are not greater than those between some of the peoples of Germany, or people in different parts of Great Britain.

Up to the sixteenth century the vast region now known as Siberia was sparsely peopled by native groups of paleo-Asiatic, Ural-Altaic, or Mongolian extraction. Most of them were more or less nomadic and in primitive states of culture. There was never any political unity, and many of the groups whose forefathers may have participated in the westward invasions had gradually lapsed into a weakened condition.

The first Russian traders crossed the Urals as early as the eleventh century, but such visits led to no consequences of importance. The conquest of Siberia began in 1580. Yermak, a Don Cossack in disgrace, really a bandit, invaded the territory east of the Urals with 1,636 followers and captured the town of Sibir. This handful of men started the conquest of a territory nearly three times as large as the whole of Russia in Europe. By 1639 Russian explorers had reached the Amur and the Pacific. The rest of Siberian history, until Soviet times, was merely a record of Russian immigration and the gradual dwindling of the natives.

Diverse Nationalities

Although Slavs account for three-quarters of the Soviet population, there are nearly 200 ethnic groups in all, at least 25 of which number half a million or more. Their nationalities and numbers are listed in the Statistical Tables. Many of these people are now mixed.

No less than 80 languages are spoken, although the main medium of communication is Russian. Most of these languages have their own literature, but several had no written records until the Soviets introduced writing and schools.

The original Lithuanian territory lay along the Baltic between the Vistula and Western Dvina, but at the time of its maximum power Lithuania's influence reached from the Gulf of Riga to the Ukraine. The Lithuanians have an admixture of all the elements surrounding them, the Poles in particular, with whom they have had long political association. From 1721 to 1918 Lithuania was a part of czarist Russia, and since 1940 has been a republic within the Soviet Union.

The Latvians, or Letts, are a mixed Baltic group related closely to the Lithuanians. From 1795 until near the end of the First World War, they were under Russia; in 1940 they became a part of the Soviet Union. The true Livonians are almost extinct. Their country lay east and north of the Gulf of Riga, and from the early part of the eleventh century the area was a bone of contention between the Russians, Germans, and Swedes. The language of the Livonians belongs to the Finno-Ugrian family, and the people are closely related to the Estonians.

The Estonians were originally a Finno-Ugrian tribe, occupying the larger part of the region of old Livonia and present Estonia. Being weaker than their neighbors, from the eleventh century on they came alternately under the influence of the Russians, Danes, Germans, and Swedes, falling in 1710 to the Russians. Estonia remained part of Russia until 1918, when it was severed from that country; in 1940 it was united with the Soviet Union.

The Finns represent the westernmost extension of the Finno-Ugrian stock. Although they have retained their language, their blood has become mixed with that of the Swedes. The more eastern population, known as the Karelians, is better preserved.

The most Mongol-like natives of Soviet Europe are the Lapps and the Samoyeds or Nentsi. Their numbers are insignificant. They occupy the northernmost limits of the Finnish and Russian territories, the Lapps extending into Scandinavia.

Turko-Tatars number approximately seven million in Soviet Europe

Many ethnic groups have gone into the Soviet melting pot. These girls are from the Kirgiz Republic (left) and the Chuvash Autonomous Republic (right). (*Courtesy U.S.S.R. National Committee, I.G.U.*)

and the Caucasus. They are divided into the Crimean Tatars, Kazan Tatars, the Bashkirs, the Chuvash, and the Kirgiz, with many minor units. They are more or less admixed and have no racial cohesion.

The Russian Jews are in the main descendants of refugees forced out of Germany during the persecutions of the Middle Ages. Some Jews penetrated into Poland and Lithuania as early as the middle of the eleventh century. They later spread to the Ukraine and Bessarabia. The total number of Jews in European Russia before the First World War approximated 4,000,000, of whom 1,300,000 were in Russian Poland. In addition, there were about 50,000 in Siberia and Middle Asia. In the 1959 census the Jews officially recorded numbered 2,268,-000.

The total number of Germans in the lands under Russian domination at the beginning of the First World War amounted to a little over 1,800,000. In 1959 the total was 1,619,000. The German influx started in the sixteenth century and was especially active during the reign of

Catherine II. Germans came as artisans and merchants, frequently on invitation, and in 1762 they were invited to settle in parts of southern Russia in agricultural colonies, especially near Saratov on the Volga. These colonies received special privileges, were practically self-governing, and fused but little with the Russians. The German landed proprietors in the Baltic provinces resulted from the attempts by German Knights to forcibly Christianize the natives and dominate the region. During the Hitler regime, most Baltic Germans were repatriated.

After the establishment of the Soviet government, the Volga Germans were organized into an Autonomous Volga German Republic. In 1941, as the invading German armies were forging eastward, the Volga group became a possible point of danger and the republic was abolished. The Germans were thus evacuated and resettled in western Siberia and Middle Asia.

A study of the prewar German relations with Russia shows that the latter has long been a field for exploitation by Germany. Care was taken by the Germans that they should not disappear into the Russian mass and thus weaken Germany to the advantage of her neighbor.

These Ukrainian or Little Russian dancers are members of the Peremog Collective Farm. (*Courtesy U.S.S.R. National Committee, I.G.U.*)

Many peoples of Middle Asia retain their colorful costumes. These Turkmen members of a collective farm near Ashkhabad are voting for their representatives in the Supreme Soviet. (*Sovfoto*)

The majority of the people in Siberia and Middle Asia today are Slavic Russians; among the rest are several groups which call for brief notice.

Since ancient times the Caucasus has been a refuge area for remnant peoples, many of whom still live in its isolated valleys. Both the Armenians and the Georgians are ancient white units, both have suffered from invasions, and both are mixed peoples. The Armenians once occupied the adjacent parts of Turkey, Iraq, and Iran. They are known from at least nine centuries before Christ, and became the first Christian nation. Armenians are famed as traders.

The Georgians, or Gruzians, are an old and important trans-Caucasian group, appearing in the twelfth century B.C. Their earliest name, curiously, was Iberians, the same as that of the people of pre-Roman Spain. Their capital, Tbilisi, dates from the middle of the first century A.D. At the beginning of the thirteenth century the country was devastated by Genghis Khan, and this was repeated in the fourteenth century by the followers of Timur. Toward the end of the eighteenth century Georgia was under the domination of Iran and Turkey; in the period 1801 to 1829 it gradually joined Russia, in part voluntarily; and in 1921 the area became a Soviet republic. Georgians constitute approximately two-thirds of the population of their republic.

The Azerbaidzhanians are about as numerous as their Georgian neighbors, and make up about the same proportion in their area.

Among the predominantly white but non-Russian people east of the Caspian are the Tadzhiks, or Tajiks. This is an old Iranian stock, mixed somewhat with the Turkmens. The Tadzhiks occupy the mountainous country near the Pamirs, and south into Afghanistan.

The Turkmens form the principal Middle Asiatic stock. They are to be counted with the Asiatic whites, but in various regions there is much mixture with the Tatars.

The main strains of the remaining Asiatic peoples are the Mongoloid in the south and the related paleo-Asiatic in the north. Among all the larger groups, especially in Uzbekistan, Kazakhstan, and Kirgiz, there are individuals whom it would be hard to class as other than whites. In the army, in physical culture parades, and in pioneer groups where all dress alike, it becomes difficult to be sure of what nationality is involved. It is principally for this reason that there is little race problem in the Soviet Union.

Aside from the larger ethnic units already mentioned, there exist many remnants of ancient tribes, in general of paleo-Asiatic or Mongolian derivation. Individuals and whole groups show close resemblances to native American Indians. These groups are known by various names, most of which were corruptions. Thus the Samoyeds are properly called Nentsi, and the Tungus are known as Evenki. In the north there are the Yakuts, speaking a Turkic language but with decidedly Mongoloid features; farther east the Chuckchee, physically the same as the Eskimo. In the southeast are small contingents of the Koreans, Japanese, Chinese, and Mongols; in the southwest live the Mongolian Kalmuks. All these groups are by now considerably admixed with Russian whites.

During the Second World War, Siberia and Middle Asia received large numbers of refugees from the Ukraine, several million in all. Whole industrial establishments with their staffs were transported. This was particularly true in the Urals, but also in Kazakhstan and Uzbekistan. Since many people have remained, these displacements have altered the population of these regions.

The statue of Peter the First overlooks the Neva River. The old Admiralty Building is to the right while the fortress of Peter and Paul with its spire lies across the
river. (*Sovfoto*)

Population Distribution

Geography is as much concerned with where people live as with
who they are. The population map is thus one of the most important
in the book. As the features of climate, soil, and agriculture are developed in other chapters, the reasons for the concentration of people
become apparent, for most settlement rests on natural factors. Most of
the people live in a triangular area bounded in the west by the Gulf of

---

POPULATION DISTRIBUTION (*map on following pages*)

Most of the Soviet people live in a roughly triangular area which lies between the
Gulf of Finland and the Black Sea, and tapers eastward into Asia. In this settled
area, which corresponds with the distribution of cultivated land, rural densities
generally exceed 50 people per square mile. In contrast, large areas to the north
and south average fewer than 5 per square mile. Urban centers show a similar
distribution.

Population patterns in Siberia and Middle Asia reflect ribbon settlement along
rivers and railways, or the presence of favorable conditions due to irrigation or
topography. Rural data from *Great Soviet World Atlas,* modified; urban data from
1959 census.

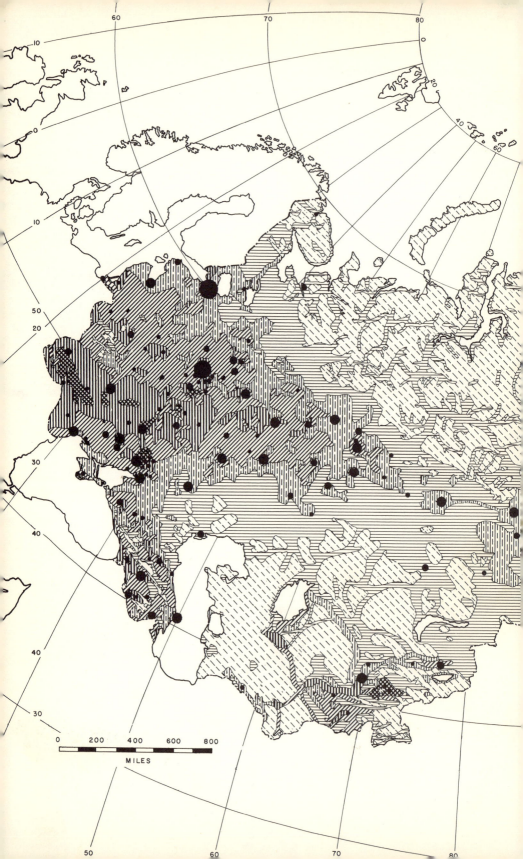

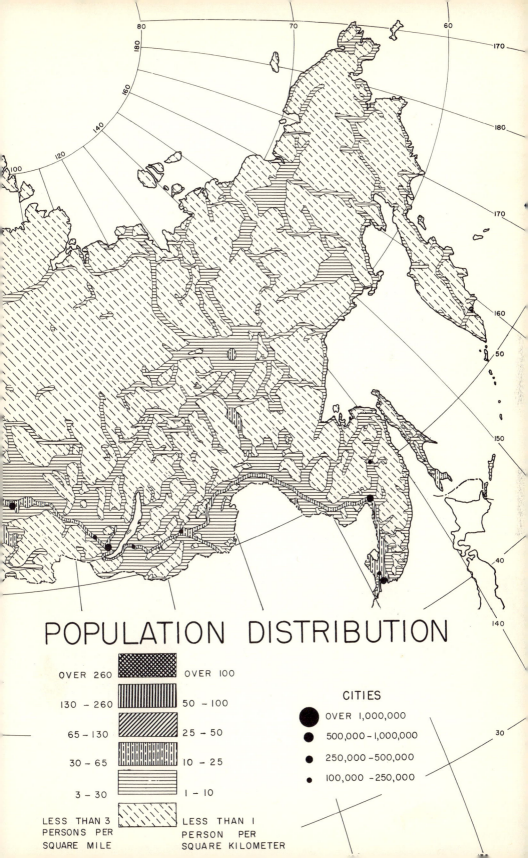

POPULATION DISTRIBUTION

OVER 260		OVER 100
130 – 260		50 – 100
65 – 130		25 – 50
30 – 65		10 – 25
3 – 30		1 – 10
LESS THAN 3 PERSONS PER SQUARE MILE		LESS THAN 1 PERSON PER SQUARE KILOMETER

CITIES

- ● OVER 1,000,000
- ● 500,000 – 1,000,000
- ● 250,000 – 500,000
- ● 100,000 – 250,000

Finland and the Black Sea, and tapering eastward into Siberia. This same area is emphasized in the maps of cultivated land and rainfall. There are scattered extensions east of Lake Baikal to the Pacific, and outliers in the fertile valleys of the Caucasus and Soviet Middle Asia.

As a result of socialist planning, cities have grown enormously. It is hard to find a center that did not double in the period between the First and Second World Wars, and many have again doubled since 1945. Moscow and Leningrad are the two giant cities, but Kiev, Baku, Gorki, Kharkov, and Tashkent approximate a million. Between this figure and half a million are two dozen cities. In 1959 the Union had 148 cities in excess of 100,000 population as against 31 in 1926 and only 14 in 1897.

With the increased emphasis on industry, new centers of concentrated population have arisen in the mining districts of the Urals, the Kuznetsk Basin, and the Kola Peninsula. Improved irrigation has added

Since the eleventh century the Red Square has been a focal point of Russian life. This old painting by Vasnetsov depicts the trading activities outside the Kremlin Walls in front of the Cathedral of St. Basil. (*Sovfoto*)

to the population in the oases of Middle Asia and along the Volga. Old industrial areas such as the Donets Basin and Moscow have grown. Everywhere urban expansion is conspicuous. Agricultural colonization is especially important in the virgin lands of southern Siberia.

It is probable that the general pattern of occupancy is well defined, and the coming decades will see only minor changes in broad outline. The center of population lies near the middle Volga, but with the development of Siberia it should gradually approach the Urals.

Local settlement patterns conform to types of land use. Where hunting, fishing, and lumbering predominate, as in the north, people live in compact clearings along rivers, for overland travel is difficult. In the cleared coniferous forest lands devoted to cereals and flax, villages are apt to be on morainic hills away from the damp valleys. In the fertile black-soil lands of the south, settlements are larger, and typically

As a result of the population explosion and increasing urbanization, every city in the Soviet Union is in the midst of a building boom, with scores of new apartment houses. Kiev has several square miles of housing such as this. (*Courtesy Soviet Embassy, Washington*)

on high stream banks. Russian villages often extend for a mile or more along a single street. Scattered farmsteads are uncommon.

Despite the huge population, there are many areas in the Soviet Union which are uninhabited. An examination of the population map at once reveals this unequal spread. Portions of the west are congested, but large parts of Siberia and Middle Asia are almost empty. About 90 per cent of the Soviet people live in one-eighth of the area; the remaining seven-eighths of the country has but 10 per cent of the population.

Racial distribution in the Soviet Union is relatively simple. Slavs occupy the bulk of eastern Europe and have spread across Siberia along railways and rivers. Turkic peoples are concentrated in Middle Asia with extensions into the Volga Valley and Yakutia. Mongol peoples live around Lake Baikal and along the lower Volga. In the extreme north and northwest are relic races such as the Finns, while the northeast has paleo-Asiatics and Tungus.

The Soviet Union is a nation of young people, most of them born since the revolution and therefore with no memories of czarism. In 1959, 65 per cent were under 30 years of age. The preponderance of young people is everywhere noticeable.

What will be the future of the Soviet people? The Russian Slavs, taken collectively, number some 160,000,000, and they are increasing yearly by a rate greater than that of any other people in Europe except some of the Balkan Slavs. Since the mass of the people belong to the rural and worker population, this increase will probably not be much reduced in the near future. This suggests that the Russians must be expected to exercise continuing world influence, both demographic and cultural.

People of many ethnic backgrounds make up the Soviet Union. This hunter, with his fur-covered skis, is from the Far East. (*Tass*)

Chapter III

LAND AND THE ECONOMY

SOVIET LANDFORMS, rainfall, temperature, soils, and minerals provide the physical basis for the nation's livelihood. Out of this environment has grown the pattern of land use, and the design of socialist economy.

Many factors help to make a nation important, including the quality of its people and the character of their tradition, government, education, and ideals. Environmental factors cover only a part of the story, and even a complete physical and cultural analysis provides but a portion of the evaluation. One contribution of geography to national welfare is to inventory and weigh the various assets and limitations; without this understanding of the environmental potential, few economic or political generalizations are possible.

Environmental Restrictions

In the Soviet Union, as in all large countries, agriculture forms an important base for the national economy. Scattered hunters or trappers may live in the northern forests, but these areas cannot support millions of people. Nomads require such large grazing areas for their animals that the population density is low. Lumbermen come and go. Miners and factory workers may create an oasis in the wilderness, fed with outside food, but mineral deposits are highly localized. Such non-

Broad plains and rich chernozem soils characterize the fields of the Lenin Collective Farm in the Krasnodar area east of the Sea of Azov. Most Soviet agriculture is now mechanized, and the former small farms have been merged into large fields. (*Courtesy Soviet Embassy, Washington*)

39

agricultural settlements seldom involve any widespread change of the landscape. The key to permanent settlement is agriculture, and farming in turn rests on climate and soil. Only where the environment is relatively favorable can the Soviet Union expect to support a dense rural population.

The Union of Soviet Socialist Republics covers eight and a half million square miles, but mere size is no assurance of strength or desirability. Great areas are too mountainous or too hilly, too cold or too hot, too dry or too wet, too infertile or too inaccessible, or otherwise un-

The peninsula of Kamchatka has the second most active volcanoes in the world, next to Java, with elevations to 16,000 feet. This peak is in the Obachinsky group. (*Courtesy U.S.S.R. National Committee, I.G.U.*)

attractive as a home for many people. An understanding of land use characteristics is basic to an evaluation of Soviet potentials.

Mountainous topography accounts for almost two million square miles; and elevations range from 24,584 feet near the Pamirs to minus 433 feet east of the Caspian Sea. Vast areas have slopes which are too steep for agricultural exploitation. High mountains rim the country on the east and south. From the Bering Straits to the Black Sea, the Soviet frontier is marked by continuous chains of mountains. Many of these are geologically young and correspondingly rugged.

Along the Pacific, Kamchatka has volcanic peaks to 16,000 feet, with the second most active volcanoes in the world. Farther inland, a complex of mountains covers all of Siberia as far as the Lena River. Within northeastern Siberia are mountain ranges up to 10,000 feet which were first explored only a few decades ago.

Mountains a mile or more in height fringe Mongolia, with elevations to three miles next to Sinkiang. The border next to Afghanistan and Iran is lower, but the mountain sequence continues to the Caspian Sea. Along the southernmost frontier lie the Pamir Mountains, known as the "roof of the world," with some of the tallest peaks on earth outside the Himalaya. Here meet the U.S.S.R., Afghanistan, Pakistan, India, and China.

The Caucasus Range rises to 18,000 feet, which is higher than the Alps. The mountains are so rugged that only three roads cross them, and the passes are often closed by snow. During the Second World War, a party of German Alpine troops scaled Mount Elbrus and planted the swastika on its summit. This marked the farthest advance of Hitler's army, for the flag was removed by the Russians a few days later.

Such a mountainous frontier provides a measure of military security, but it equally bars trade and easy access for people and ideas. One

---

GEOMORPHIC REGIONS (*map on following pages*)

Within the 8,650,000 square miles of Soviet territory is a wide range of elevation and of land form. Plains and low hills characterize the western half, with mountains and high hills in the east and south. The map recognizes 18 major geomorphic regions and a total of 85 subdivisions.

Soviet Europe extends to the eastern base of the Ural Uplands and the northern foothills of the Caucasian Highlands. Middle Asia lies between the Black Sea and the borders of China, and on the north takes in the Caspian Depression, the Turgai Plain, and the Kazakh Upland. Siberia occupies two-thirds of the total area, but accounts for only one-seventh of the population.

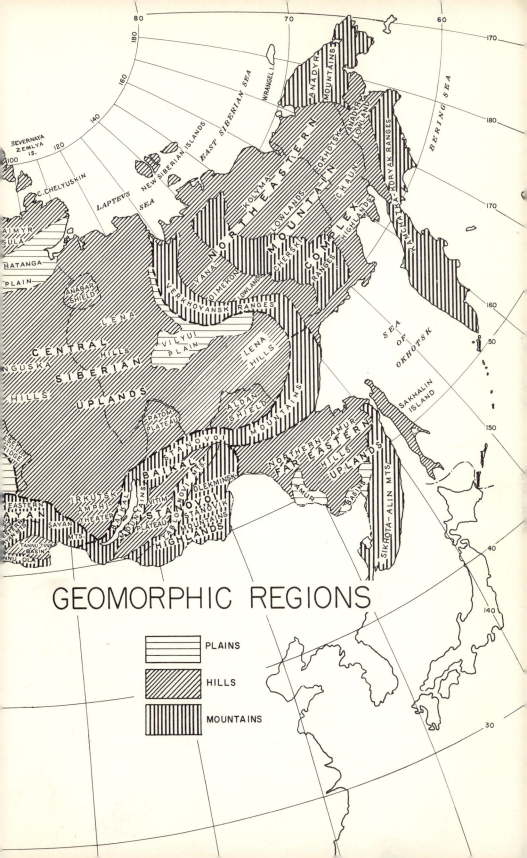

GEOMORPHIC REGIONS

PLAINS

HILLS

MOUNTAINS

cannot evaluate Soviet strategy nor understand its cultural history without an appreciation of these rugged topographic barriers. Only in the west is the U.S.S.R. approachable across level land.

Only one important mountain range lies within the interior of the Union, the low and rounded Urals. The Urals are an undramatic line of mountains. In the center, where they are crossed by several railways, elevations are no more than one or two thousand feet. Farther north and south, peaks reach a mile in height. Nowhere are there steep slopes or rugged topography. These mountains provide a faint excuse for any line separating Europe and Asia, for the Urals mark no basic change in climate, vegetation, agriculture, people, or politics. If there is something to be called "Asia," it is not noticeable here.

It may be helpful to realize that the Urals are surprisingly like the Appalachians. Both are long and narrow, both are low in the center but rise to a mile in the north and south. Both have hill country to the west; both have a piedmont on their east. The difference is that the Urals are far more richly mineralized, due perhaps to their deeper erosion.

In addition to the mountainous area of the Union, lands which are too hilly for normal cultivation cover another million square miles. Both mountains and hills are areas of steep slopes where agriculture is sharply limited by topography, regardless of whether or not the climate is suitable. The difference between a hill and a mountain is merely in the local height or relief. Both are sloping lands; in fact, some hills are more sharply dissected than some mountains. Mountains have a local relief of a thousand feet or more; hills are measured in tens or hundreds of feet.

Most of central Siberia between the Yenisei and the Lena rivers is thoroughly hilly. There is also hill country in Middle Asia and in the Ukraine. Much of the Ural area is hilly land. West of Moscow are the low Valdai Hills, historically important as a barrier to invading armies. Hills also characterize the area next to Finland.

Lands which have too short a growing season for agriculture occupy between three and four million square miles in the north and east; in other words, nearly half of the eight and a half million square miles of the Union is too cold. Much of Siberia has the shortest frost-free season and the lowest temperatures of any inhabited area in the world. Temperature data for two stations show January day and night averages of −57° F. and −67° F., and Verkhoyansk has recorded a record low of −92.3° F. People can live in such situations only because

Long and severe winters characterize vast areas in the north, and the frost-free growing season lasts for less than three months. This scene is from the Nentsi National Okrug. (*Tass*)

the winter air is dry, and because these extreme temperatures occur only on calm days; when the wind blows the temperature rises.

It is not the extremely low winter temperatures which restrict cultivation, but rather the brief period between the last frost in the spring and the first freezing days in the fall, combined with the low temperatures during the growing season.

Most field crops require a growing season of a hundred days, or at least three months free from frost before maturity. Areas of short summers are also areas of variable summers; one cannot count on growing seasons of equal length. One Siberian town which averages 90 frost-free days had two successive years in which the period varied from 75 to 125 days.

An irregular line from Leningrad to southern Lake Baikal and the Amur River marks the northern limit of feasible cultivation. To the north are a few favored areas and some untypical experiment stations, but there is little prospect of widespread farming. Experiment stations north of the Arctic Circle actually raise potatoes, but most of them are no bigger than walnuts. If new varieties of wheat or other grains can be developed which will mature in eighty days, cultivation may advance tens of miles northward, but not even the most enthusiastic Russian agriculturalist predicts that the Arctic area will ever be extensively cultivated or thickly settled.

Large parts of the eastern Soviet Union are underlain by permanently frozen ground, areas where the soil never thaws more than a few feet. This is an inheritance from the glacial period, except that Siberia had no ice sheet. In the absence of any blanket of snow, intense radiation cooled the earth. Soviet scientists have made detailed studies of this permafrost, and find that it extends to depths of hundreds of feet; in a few places the ground is permanently frozen for two thousand feet. During the brief summer, the surface may thaw to a depth of five or even ten feet. At one point in the Arctic, at the end of the summer, the writer found ice crystals only a foot and a half below the surface. Agriculture is obviously restricted where the ground is so cold. More than three and a half million square miles of northern Asia is underlain by this permanently frozen ground, an area as large as the entire United States.

It is easier to define land which is too cold for crops than that which is too hot. Part of the problem with high temperatures is that evaporation becomes excessive. Since these hot lands lie in the desert, not much water is available to begin with. Areas in Soviet Middle Asia regularly reach 110° F., and a temperature of 122° F. has been recorded. These high temperatures, exceptional for these latitudes, reflect the extreme continentality and seasonality of interior Asia. High summer temperatures combine with rapid evaporation to render several hundred thousand square miles agriculturally unproductive. Even if abundant water were available, agriculture would face difficulties of excessive transpiration.

Growing seasons which are too short and temperatures which are too low are even more of a limiting factor on agriculture than unfavorable land forms. About half of the Soviet Union has temperature restrictions of one kind or another.

Vast areas of the Soviet Union are too dry for successful farming. American agriculture requires at least 20 inches of rain for normal cultivation. This 20-inch rainfall line forms a boundary which runs northward from the mouth of the Rio Grande through central Kansas and the central Dakotas. To the west of that line farming is uncertain.

In the Soviet Union, with its higher latitudes and lower temperatures, 20 inches of rainfall "goes further" since temperatures are lower and evaporation is less. The Russians cultivate down to the 15-inch rainfall

Nearly two million square miles of Soviet territory are too dry for normal agriculture. This irrigation system diverts water from the Chu River near Frunze. (*Tass*)

PRECIPITATION (*map on following pages*)

Much of the Soviet Union is relatively dry, a product of its remoteness from the moisture-contributing ocean, barrier mountains, and atmospheric circulation.

The Arctic Ocean is frozen for much of the year so that it yields little moisture by evaporation, and the Indian Ocean is an ineffective source for Soviet precipitation due to intervening mountains. The Pacific contributes monsoon rainfall to the Far East, but such moisture rarely penetrates beyond Lake Baikal. The Atlantic is thus the only feasible source for rain or snow, and it is far distant from the heart of the country. Mountains such as the Caucasus or Sayan extract extra precipitation through their orographic influence.

A comparable map of the United States would show almost twice the average rainfall.

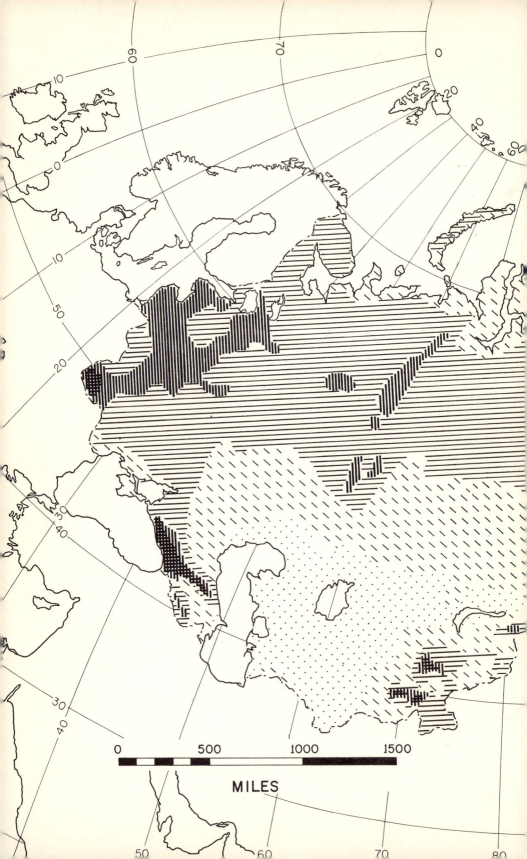

MILES

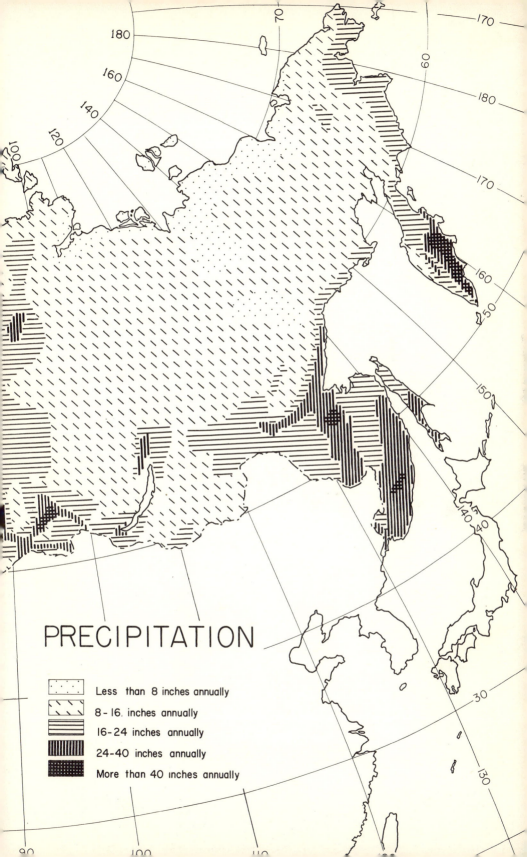

PRECIPITATION

Less than 8 inches annually

8-16 inches annually

16-24 inches annually

24-40 inches annually

More than 40 inches annually

line, or even the 12-inch boundary, but with increasing hazard. Variability in rainfall becomes more and more pronounced with lower annual totals. A statistical average of 12 inches may mean 8 one year, 5 the next, and 23 the next; one cannot even be sure of 120 inches in a decade.

Nearly two million square miles, a quarter of Soviet territory, average less than 12 inches of precipitation. All of this area is either desert or semi-desert, most of it unusable for cultivation and some of it unattractive for grazing. Here and there are oases, fed by streams which rise in snow-covered mountains, but these are only small spots on the map. The great proportion of this dry country will probably remain desolate and empty. The Soviets have ambitious plans for irrigation and drought control, but the obstacles are impressive.

The area which is too dry for safe agriculture, and which thus has but scanty population, begins in the southern Ukraine, includes the land along the lower Volga and around the Caspian Sea, and continues across Soviet Middle Asia to the borders of the Mongolian Desert.

Poor drainage characterizes many lowland plains, in part due to flat terrain, in part a result of glacial conditions. Drainage ditches have reclaimed large areas. (*Courtesy Soviet Embassy, Washington*)

In contrast to this area of drought is a small area which is too wet. There is not much of such wet land, but to continue the sequence of land which is to be eliminated from settlement because of environmental handicaps, it is proper to record an area which receives 100 inches of rain. This is on the slopes of the Caucasus Mountains at the eastern end of the Black Sea. If there were no run-off or evaporation, such rainfall would create a lake eight feet deep each year.

Still other areas are too swampy, as in the glaciated lands of Byelorussia or the northern Ob valley. Elsewhere many soils are too acid or too alkaline to be productive.

Soviet Climate

The climate of the Soviet Union is dominated by a parade of low and high pressure areas which move eastward across the country about once a week. These migrating cyclonic and anticyclonic storms draw in great masses of cold air from the Arctic, especially in winter, and in the absence of barrier mountains this polar air extends to the mountains along the southern frontiers. Sheltered areas behind the mountains of the Crimea or the Caucasus, or protected valleys within the Pamirs, thus have a subtropical climate.

Little moisture is imported from the Arctic seas, and the Pacific lies on the lee side of the continent and only contributes monsoon-type rains to the eastern edges of Siberia. Tibet and the highlands of inner Asia clearly prevent the Indian Ocean from being more than a negligible contributor of moisture. This leaves only the Atlantic as an effective source of rain, brought into the interior by the parade of passing storms. With increasing distance from the sea, rainfall diminishes, and

---

CLIMATIC REGIONS (*map on following pages*)

Cold and/or drought characterize Soviet climates. The Koeppen system of classification recognizes four main types within the U.S.S.R.: *ET* or polar tundra climate, *D* climate with short summers and long severe winters, *C* climate with long hot summers and mild winters, and *B* or dry climates of either the steppe or *BS* type or of desert character known as *BW*.

These major groups are further classified as:

a, hot summers with the warmest month averaging over 72° F.;

b, cool summers with four months above 50° F.;

c, short cool summers with one to three months above 50° F.;

d, severe winters with the coldest month below -36° F.

t, moist throughout the year;

s, dry summers;

w, dry winters

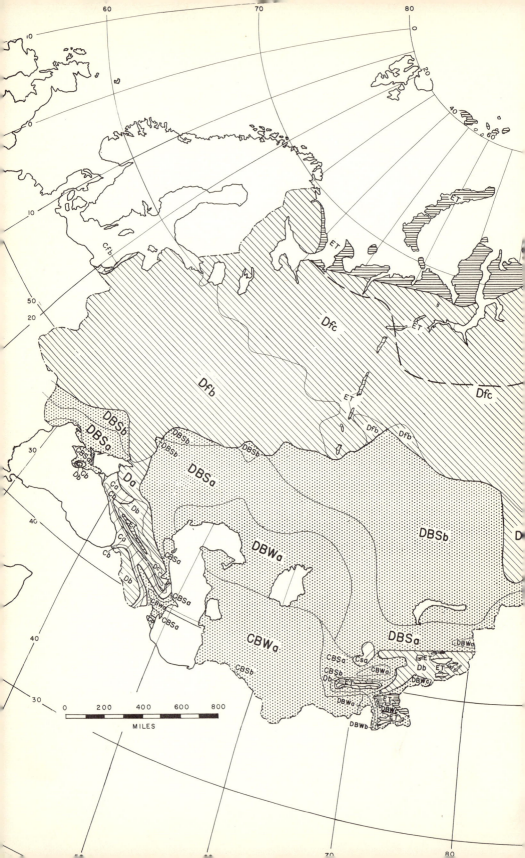

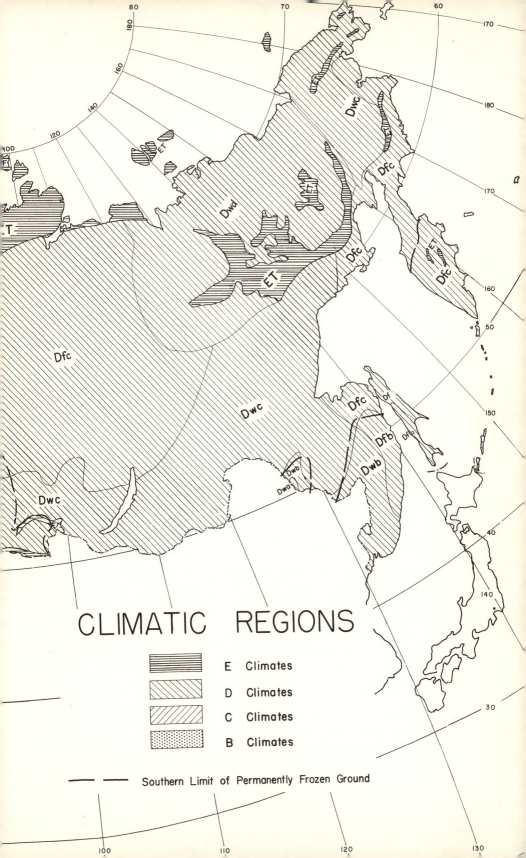

CLIMATIC REGIONS

	E Climates
	D Climates
	C Climates
	B Climates

— — — Southern Limit of Permanently Frozen Ground

only adiabatic cooling on the highest mountain slopes can produce heavy precipitation from the nearly dry air.

Not only does the Soviet Union extend for thousands of miles from west to east, but the extent in latitude is equally impressive. The southern limits lie within 12 degrees of the tropics, while the northernmost part of the continent is within 12 degrees of the Pole. The south scarcely has a winter, the north barely experiences summer. Frost is as rare in Turkestan as are hot days in Cape Chelyuskin, 3,000 miles to the north.

Spring begins near the Afghan border in late January, where the year-round climate is so subtropical that date palms flourish and snow is uncommon. In March and April, the warm sun of spring shines on Kazakhstan, and the desert is carpeted with red tulips and poppies. As winter retreats northward, the steppes of the central U.S.S.R. are free from snow and are covered with a mass of spring flowers by early May. Moscow has apple blossoms in late May, three months later than the far south. Spring does not reach northern Siberia until June; then the ice leaves the rivers and the tundra blooms. Near the Arctic Ocean frost may occur as late as August, so that spring, summer, and fall are only momentary phenomena.

Four main climatic areas may be recognized in terms of the Koeppen classification, as outlined in the map of Climatic Regions. These are the tundra or ET type near the Arctic, the very extensive array of D or cool temperate climates which characterize most of the central area, and the steppe or BS and the desert or BW types of the southwest.

Tundra climates are characterized by long winters. Temperatures are not so low as those in the interior, but the frost-free summer may last but one or two months. The precipitation is 8 to 12 inches, in places no more than in the southern deserts, but the presence of permanently frozen ground prevents subsurface drainage and leads to widespread swamps. While true tundra climates are limited to the Arctic coastal lowlands, comparable conditions occur farther south at progressively higher elevations.

Cool temperate climates characterize most of the U.S.S.R. Winters are long and severe, the coldest on earth outside polar areas. In contrast, the short summers usually have a few uncomfortably warm days. Spring and fall are only brief transition periods during the rapid shift between the main seasons. Precipitation occurs throughout the year, except toward the Pacific where the summer monsoon brings a rainfall maximum, with considerable fog and drizzle. The rainfall is everywhere limited, as befitting the continental interior. The amount varies from 21 inches at Moscow or 19 inches at Leningrad, to 20 inches at Tomsk, and less eastward. The tempering influence of the Atlantic

Ocean creates a roughly triangular area in European Russia where summers have four months above 50° F. in contrast to three months or less elsewhere. Pacific influence forms a much smaller mild area in the extreme southeast.

Steppe climates receive rainfall of 8 to 16 inches. They occur in the Ukraine and Middle Asia, where summers are hot, with one or more months averaging over 72° F. Evaporation is excessive, so that the soil is usually dry. Winters are very cold, due to the invasion of polar air masses from Siberia. Such conditions are found eastward from the Black Sea across the southern Ukraine to Lake Balkhash. Strong northerly winds blow for much of the year, reaching gale force during the winter *burans*. In summer, hot dry air may stream westward, known as the *sukhovey*.

Deserts, in this case with 8 inches of rain or less, cover a large area east of the Caspian Sea. Summers everywhere are very hot. Toward the north winters are cold, but south of the Aral Sea warmer conditions prevail. Clear skies accompany the low humidity.

In addition to these four climatic regions, mild C climates prevail in the Caucasus and the humid parts of Soviet Middle Asia, where temperature and rainfall vary with altitude.

It is clear that large parts of the Union are relatively unattractive for settlement. Vast areas, perhaps as much as six or seven million square miles in all, may long remain nearly empty. Maps become meaningful only as one appreciates the features which they show; no one should look at the total Soviet landscape without an awareness of the vast areas which are undesirable as a home for man.

The Agricultural Triangle

How much good land remains after unfavorable areas have been eliminated, and where is it located? Most of the land which is not too steep, or too cold, or too dry, or otherwise unfavorable, lies largely within an irregular triangle which tapers eastward into Asia. This measures roughly a million square miles, or almost one-eighth of the entire Union. Along the north the good land is roughly bounded by a line from the Baltic Sea near Leningrad to Irkutsk and southern Lake Baikal; on the south it is limited by a line from Odessa on the Black Sea to Lake Baikal. Since the tapering end of the triangle is discontinuous, the eastern limit of continuous cultivation lies near Krasnoyarsk on the Yenisei River. On the west, the favorable agricultural area continues across Poland and Germany to France.

This agricultural wedge is the essential core of the country. In origin it reflects the diminishing influence of moisture from the Atlantic Ocean. Here is the basic reason for the Soviet pattern of population distribution. To the north of the agricultural triangle, summers are too short for cultivation; to the south, rainfall is too low. Other small areas of usable land lie in Middle Asia and along the Amur Valley toward the Pacific, but nine-tenths of all the farms and people are within the triangle. The same is true for railways and industrial cities. Here is the heart of the nation.

Out of the eight and a half million square miles in the entire country, the one million square miles within the triangle represents the major area with attractive agricultural possibilities. Not all of this is usable for cultivation, for much has poor soil, or bad drainage, or is rough terrain. The land which actually grows food—the net crop area— covers less than 600,000 square miles, some 7 per cent of the country. This half million or more square miles is slightly larger than the cultivated area in the United States, but when the latter numbered 180,-000,000 people, the Soviets had a population of 220,000,000. Much more important, the over-all quality of American farmland is far superior to that in the U.S.S.R.

Whereas the United States has been able to produce larger and larger yields from progressively smaller areas, the Soviets have had to add additional farmland. This has been obtained from drainage of swamps, irrigation of desert borders, and cultivation of steppe areas through dry-farming techniques. These added as much as 100,000 square miles during the 1950's.

Poor soils and marginal climate will long handicap the Soviet food supply. Despite prospects for new varieties of grain, better fertilizers, and new machines, the permanent handicaps of the Soviet Union appear so limiting that it seems doubtful whether the people of the U.S.S.R. can ever be as well fed as those of the United States. Soviet restrictions of poor soil, limited rainfall, and short growing season seem to create severe limitations on the food supply. As two American agriculturists have written:

> Russia has never been, is not now, and probably never can become a really great and dependable producer of food grains, such as the United States whose corn production alone equals in food value all of the grains produced in the land of the Soviets.[*]

[*] Truog, Emil and Pronin, Dimitri T., "A Great Myth: The Russian Granary," *Land Economics*, XXIX, p. 200 (1953).

There is no question that the Soviets are making great improvements in their agriculture, and will continue to do so. What is equally clear, however, is that they face major environmental restrictions. Even within the area now cultivated there is land poorer than the New England hillsides which were abandoned a century ago, or poorer than fields in the dry American Southwest which should be kept in pasture.

Soviet agriculture has two frontiers, whereas the United States has but one. To the north is the frontier of cold, where cultivation pushes into lands of shorter and shorter summers; here frost is a constant danger. To the south is a frontier of aridity, where agriculture advances into lands with less and less rainfall, so that occasional crop failure due to drought is inevitable.

The pattern of population and the location of the agricultural triangle provide a clue to many Soviet problems. This is shown in the history of old Russia. For centuries settlement has pushed eastward into Asia. On maps which show the extent of agriculture century by century, one may trace this advancing wedge as it has been driven farther and farther into the continental interior. As agriculture has advanced eastward, pioneering settlement has pushed northward into the forest and southward into the steppe. Here is the evolving pattern of Russian colonization. It is interesting to note that the Trans-Siberian Railway roughly follows the middle of the agricultural triangle; its surveyors had a sound understanding of settlement possibilities.

How much farther can this wedge of settlement be pushed? With local exceptions, the present extent of agriculture appears to be near the limit with the techniques now available. The point of the triangle is dented against the mountains of central Siberia. North and south, cultivation has already invaded areas so marginal in their crop potentials that poor harvests are recurrent. In terms of environmental possibilities and unless there are major changes in techniques, it seems probable that the limits of agricultural Russia at the end of the century will have much the same pattern as today. Where virgin land cultivation in Siberia has been successful it has been near the dry southern margin of the triangle; where it has failed it has been too close to the desert.

What does the map reveal? Is the Union of Soviet Socialist Republics an Asiatic or a European country? The present orientation is clearly toward the west, with the economic center of gravity somewhere near the middle Volga. The Soviet Union has a long coastline on the Pacific, and this will surely increase in importance, but the Pacific will long remain the country's back door. The Soviet Far East has little in common with California, nor even with Alaska; Pacific Siberia is like Canada's Labrador.

The over-all orientation of the Soviet Union was demonstrated during both World Wars. Let us suppose that during the Second World War Japan had ventured to invade Siberia, and that they had been successful. How far would any invading army have to move overland before it could achieve real victory? Lake Baikal is 2,000 miles from the Pacific, but this is only the apex of the fertile triangle. It is true that there are cities and industry in the Soviet Far East, but their loss would not be fatal. An invasion of 4,000 miles would only reach the Urals, and would certainly not be enough to cause the country to surrender. Air power introduces new strategic concepts, but distances and the location of critical areas remain.

On the other hand, when Napoleon, the Kaiser, and Hitler advanced from the west, they occupied the thick end of the triangle. The Russians thus lost a large part of their food supply and their leading industrial areas. A penetration of less than 1,000 miles brought the Germans to Volgagrad, formerly Stalingrad,* but even this was not enough to achieve victory.

To invade and occupy the vast territory of the U.S.S.R. is about the most difficult military assignment imaginable, even in the air age. Such a feat would presumably require the occupation of the Ukraine, the Volga Valley, and the Urals. A logistical task of comparable difficulty would be for a foreign power to occupy Pittsburgh and Chicago.

Geography appears to have placed serious limitations on the development of the Soviet Union. Man can do much, but the restrictions of great distances, remoteness from the ocean, unfavorable terrain, short growing seasons, inadequate and variable rainfall, and continentality will long remain. Only the one million square miles of the agricultural triangle are relatively favorable, and only half of this is actually cultivated.

The Soviet Union is big; here is a nation of continental proportions, nearly three times the area of the United States. Size is indeed an asset, but mere bigness is no guarantee of national importance.

Planned Economy

When Russia emerged from the First World War and the Revolution of 1917, a thousand things needed attention. There were serious shortages in food, clothing, housing, and many necessities. Instead of providing these essentials of livelihood, the government turned its

---

* In 1961 all cities previously named after Joseph Stalin were renamed. Stalingrad became Volgagrad, Stalinsk is now Novo Kuznetsk, Stalino is Donets, and Stalinabad is renamed Dushanbe.

attention to basic production, heavy industry, and transport. The leaders of the Soviet Union proposed to create the world's first socialized state, and to achieve this utopian goal personal needs were sacrificed. Such an objective appeared to them so desirable that they regarded themselves as humanitarians, strange as that appeared to the outside world.

The map of Russia in the second half of the twentieth century is very different from that of earlier decades. Great changes have taken place, and others may be expected. It is not merely that cities have grown and railroads have been built. In many places and in many ways the face of nature has been altered. Soviet economy proposes to modify the environment wherever necessary; here is its most audacious challenge.

Soviet planning finds its basis in the supposed logic of dialectic materialism. Karl Marx and his followers conceived of society as in a constant process of modification. These changes are presumed to proceed according to fixed materialistic principles, i.e., political transition from feudalism through capitalism and socialism to a communist economy. Only in step with these ideological changes can society be correspondingly modified.

The natural environment is also thought to be a variable, and the power to direct its development depends on the stage of man's political evolution. Soviet planning is thus thought to have unique tools for the reshaping of nature and the redistribution of productive forces. Changes are said to be possible under state socialism which cannot be achieved under capitalist economy. Whereas everyone recognizes man's ability to modify nature, one may question the Soviet line that control is possible only under a Marxian system.

Socialist ability to reshape nature presumes the alteration of any natural situations which restrict crop production or economic development. Thus drought, or poor soils, or short growing seasons are all thought to be susceptible to communist improvements. Liabilities are to be changed into assets. The possibilities are thus limitless, and the place of geography in state planning becomes obvious.

Socialist economy proceeds according to an organized plan wherein the various items of production and consumption are all tied together. This means that the output of shoes, or the yield of cotton and wheat, is determined some years in advance and integrated into the total planned economy. To plan, one must predict, and to predict with accuracy, one must control. Hence the justification for stern police measures where people do not cooperate.

It is one thing to plan the production of so many tons of coal or

The labor supply is still a large factor in Soviet harvests. These women are on the "Victory" state farm near Gorki. (*Tass*)

steel rails some years hence; it is something else to assure a fixed output of agricultural products where climatic variables are involved. To count on a specific crop yield a year in advance means that one must forecast the weather and arrange for special corrective measures in case rainfall or temperatures are to be abnormal. This is what is meant by controlling nature.

The more audacious Soviet agriculturalists would push the limits of cultivation northward almost to the Arctic Circle, and south into the deserts where there is but eight inches of rainfall. The hazards and uncertainties are usually passed over by the assertion that socialist methods, in contrast to capitalist techniques, can assure planned harvests irrespective of variations in the weather. The planners thus hope that in dry areas shelterbelt planting will modify the basic climate, and that

Mechanization has enabled the Union to expand its crop acreage and release rural manpower for urban needs. This poor stand of wheat reflects the limited rainfall of Azerbaidzhan. (*Tass*)

engineering works will change the course of rivers. Man is thus to be freed from the vagaries of fluctuating crop yields or natural restrictions.

When the author delivered a paper on the deserts of Asia before an international congress in Moscow, one Russian comment was that whereas deserts may still exist in capitalistic societies, "communism can eliminate deserts in a single Five Year Plan."

The Soviet Union now operates under a socialist economy; true communism is for the future. Private initiative is entirely eliminated. The productive capacities of the state and the work of its citizens are devoted to those undertakings and in those places which are approved in the general plan. Production goals are not always fulfilled, but the successive and generally successful Five Year Plans have made it clear that the U.S.S.R. has great capacity to meet high aims. Giant steel mills, thousands of miles of new railways and oil pipe lines, mechanized agriculture, rebuilt cities, and improved livelihood all testify to the ability of the government to achieve large material goals.

At the same time, it seems obvious that the Union faces major environmental handicaps, and that there are practical restrictions beyond which it is not feasible to go. The geographic limitations of cold, drought, poor terrain, and inaccessibility will persist.

The ultimate limit to man's use of the earth lies in his ingenuity and the amount of effort which he is prepared to invest. But it should be clear that with the same skill and investment, the returns will be larger in more favorable environments. The United States of America enjoys assets of climate, soil, resources, and location which seem to outweigh those of the Union of Soviet Socialist Republics. If the two peoples have equal technical ability, patriotism, and determination, the United States should keep in the lead. The only way in which the Soviet Union can overtake America is by more sacrifice and harder work than the latter cares to invest.

If it is true that the Soviet Union wishes to avoid another world war, one reason for this attitude is the narrowing gap between socialist and capitalist production. In their desire to expand industry rapidly, the Soviets plow back a large part of the profits into further plant investment rather than devoting them to consumer welfare. Even if the government should want war, it would seem to their advantage to postpone it as long as possible.

While Soviet development during the mid-century years was spectacular, it must be remembered that the U.S.S.R. and the U.S.A. started from a very different base. Whereas the United States has already passed out of the expansion period in cropland and transport which followed the Civil War of a century ago, the Soviet Union still needs more farm land and more railways. A major factor in Soviet gains was the growth of her industrial manpower. During the Five Year Plans, Soviet factories absorbed workers at the rate of two million a year, but this drained off so many agricultural workers that crop yields were imperiled. No such fresh labor force is now available.

To Westerners, one of the surprising aspects of all Soviet cities is the small size of the commercial core. Private business is replaced by state stores, but the volume of retail trade is limited. The Union has concentrated on heavy industry and producer goods rather than on clothing, food, and consumer items. As a result, a city of 200,000 people has a smaller quantity and a much smaller variety of merchandise than a West European city of one-tenth its size. Many basic commodities which are elsewhere regarded as essential are here almost unknown.

Russian villages have even less in the way of commercial activities. Settlements of several hundred houses may have no store, for people live a nearly self-sufficient existence.

The Soviet consumer has indeed been patient; each time a new Five Year Plan was announced, people were promised that while this one must concern basic industry and defense, next time consumer goods would be included. So effective is Soviet propaganda that people have been persuaded to enjoy the fragrance of a promised flower while it is still a dirty bulb.

The U.S.S.R. began its first Seven Year Plan in 1959. Earlier Five Year programs, dating from 1928, had already transformed the map of the country and advanced the Union to a significant place in world economy. Between 1959 and 1965 the Seven Year Plan proposed to double industrial production, increase the harvest of grain by one-quarter, greatly enlarge retail trade, and increase rail freight one-third. While the labor force was to expand only slightly, its productivity was scheduled for a major increase.

As pointed out in the official directives, "The main task of the Seven Year Plan for the development of the Soviet state economy for 1959–1965 is the further intensive development of all branches of the economy based primarily on the growth of heavy industry, and a considerable strengthening of the country's economic potential in order to secure a stable increase in the national standard of living."

The goal of the successive plans has been to give balanced attention to all parts of the country, with the implication that czarist developments neglected the outlying areas. It is still apparent, however, that the major center of economic consumption lies in the west, and that the bulk of Siberia remains undeveloped.

For the 1959–1965 period, 40 per cent of the capital input was to be devoted to the "eastern regions," apparently referring to the Urals, Siberia, and Middle Asia. At the end of the period this eastern area was to produce 50 per cent of the coal, 30 per cent of the oil, 46 per cent of the electricity, 48 per cent of the steel, and 45 per cent of the lumber and forest products. Its share of the population was to remain under 20 per cent.

Each of the Plans has involved large increases in production. Expressed in somewhat vague units, the 1965 goal is a national income of sixty-six times that of 1913. The dramatic increase in electric power is a case in point. Expressed in kilowatt-hours, the 1928 production was 5 billion; this rose in 1940 to 48.3 billion and in 1950 to 91.2 billion. Data for the beginning and end of the Seven Year Plan, 1958–1965, were 233.4 and 500 billion. The 1975 goal is 1,500 billion kilowatt-hours.

In world terms, Russia's industrial output is supposed to have grown from 3 per cent of the world total in 1917 to 20 per cent in 1958. One

High mountains border the Union from the Black Sea to Bering Strait. This is a view of the Caucasus along the Georgian Military Highway. (*Photo by M. Trakhman*)

may question the basis for such statistics, but the real point is that major changes have taken place. In basic mineral production and in heavy industry, the Soviet Union now stands second only to the United States. What was once a backward agrarian country is today a great industrial power.

Chapter IV

MINERAL RESOURCES

FEW NATIONS have ever made such spectacular economic changes in so brief a period as the Soviet Union. Within half a lifetime Russia has advanced from a backward agrarian country to one of the world's foremost industrial nations. Without vast mineral deposits, plus consistent effort, this would have been impossible; few countries are more fortunate in these respects. If the environmental picture of the previous chapter presents serious limitations, the story of minerals is more favorable.

When the Soviets inaugurated their first Five Year Plan, they recognized that heavy industry must rest on mining, and that mining in turn depends on geological surveys. As a result, the Union has given close attention to the mapping of its terrain. In several years during the mid-century period, the annual exploration budget was equivalent to 1 per cent of the gross national product.

The Soviet Union is so large that all of the geological survey has not been completed, but the general picture is clear. This is a land with great mineral wealth, second only to the United States in its natural resources and perhaps even in first place. At the same time it is well to emphasize the wide gap between undeveloped theoretical potentials, still untested, and actual mineral production fabricated into machinery.

The rich mineral deposits of the U.S.S.R. have enabled the country to become the world's second industrial state. This is a view of the high-speed continuous strip mill at the Zaporozhe steel works in the Ukraine. (*Sovfoto*)

Industrial Strength

What makes a nation great, and how does one measure its potential? Does the Soviet Union have the basic resources to become the world's number one power? These pages attempt to evaluate some of the mineral resource factors.

It is obvious that in industrial strength the Soviet Union has come a long way from the status of czarist Russia at the beginning of the century. The question for the moment is how much further the country can go.

Some aspects of Soviet production are slipshod or inadequate, but a few things have been done exceptionally well. Steel plants at Novo Kuznetsk and at Magnitogorsk are among the world's best, and the Krivoi Rog blast furnace is the world's largest. When the Soviets decided to explore outer space, their sputniks were the first, and they were the first to put a man into orbit. The Moscow, Leningrad, and Kiev subways are surely the world's most ornate. In general, Soviet mines are in good shape, with electric lights, modern machinery, and expanding production. Russia is in a hurry, and it is not surprising that some things have been done poorly, or that others have had to wait.

One major limitation on the steel industry in some areas is the absence near by of coking coal suitable for use in blast furnaces. Suitable metallurgical coal must be brought hundreds of miles for use in the giant steel mills at Magnitogorsk, Nizhni Tagil, and elsewhere.

Modern industry demands an increasing array of raw materials. Some may be imported, provided that the necessary foreign currency is available, but unless most of the tonnage commodities are produced at home, industrial progress is seriously handicapped. Furthermore, the mere possession of these resources does not guarantee greatness; the material assets which now make the Soviet Union rich have been present for centuries; it is their development which counts.

The economic geology of the U.S.S.R. is reasonably well known. New discoveries are continually being made, but the basic story is clear: It is an established certainty that the Soviet Union is a tremendously rich country. In variety, its mineral wealth probably exceeds that of the United States. The Soviet Union does not have everything it needs, but more nearly than any other country it is a self-sufficient national unit. This is an asset of great significance.

An analysis of Soviet mineral developments by a Committee of the United States Congress reads as follows:

As a result of this work, the U.S.S.R. now claims possession of commercial reserves of all mineral commodities including diamonds. It further claims the world's largest explored reserves of iron ore (41 per cent of the world total), manganese ore (88 per cent of world total), copper, lead, zinc, nickel, bauxite, tungsten, mercury, mica, potash salts (54 per cent of world total), peat (60 per cent of world total), coal (53 per cent of world total geological reserves), and significant resources of crude petroleum, natural gas, phosphate raw material (nearly one-third of world total explored reserves), titanium, molybdenum, uranium, sulfur, and numerous other minerals. There is insufficient quantitative data on the individual commodities to support these Soviet claims to such vast mineral resources . . . However, the U.S.S.R., if for no other reason than its immense size, undoubtedly possesses great mineral wealth. . . . *

Sources of Power

Within the Soviet Union are four major sources of power: coal, oil, atomic energy, and hydroelectricity. The last is considered in the following chapter. For data, see Statistical Tables.

Over-all Soviet energy potentials have been evaluated by another United States Congressional Committee as follows:

The primary energy reserves of the U.S.S.R., exclusive of hydro-electric resources, are estimated at almost 7 trillion metric tons of standard fuel. (Standard fuel has a calorific value of 7,000 kilocalories

* U.S. Congress, Senate Committee on Interior and Insular Affairs, *Mineral Resources of and Background Information on the Eastern Hemisphere*, pp. 26–27. Washington, D.C. (Dec. 1958).

NATURAL RESOURCES (*map on following pages*)

The Soviet Union has vast undeveloped resources; this map is limited to those actually in production. Three great mining areas stand out: the Ukraine with its coal, iron, and manganese, the Urals with their vast array of metals and with near-by oil, and the Kuznetsk Basin in Central Siberia with its coal. Hydroelectricity is adding an impressive source of power, although still less than that from thermal electricity.

The size of the symbols suggests the relative importance of production; thus the gold fields of eastern Siberia are of first world rank, as are the new oil fields between the Urals and the Volga.

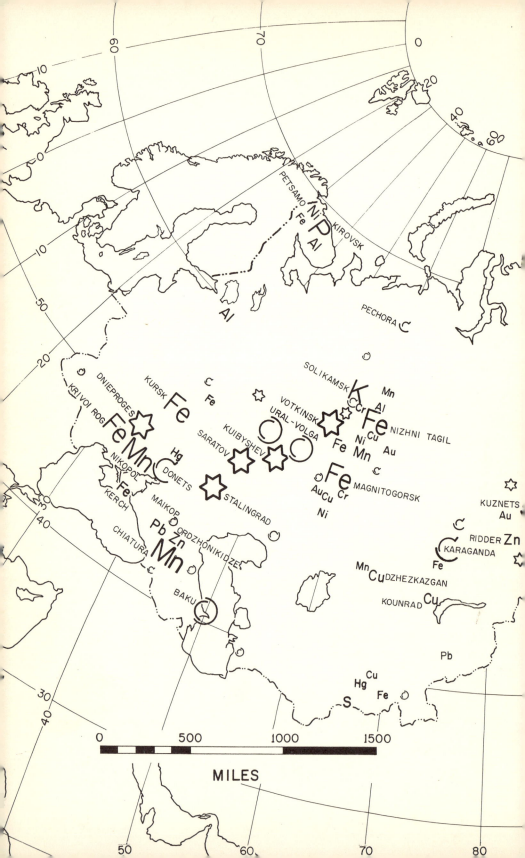

MILES

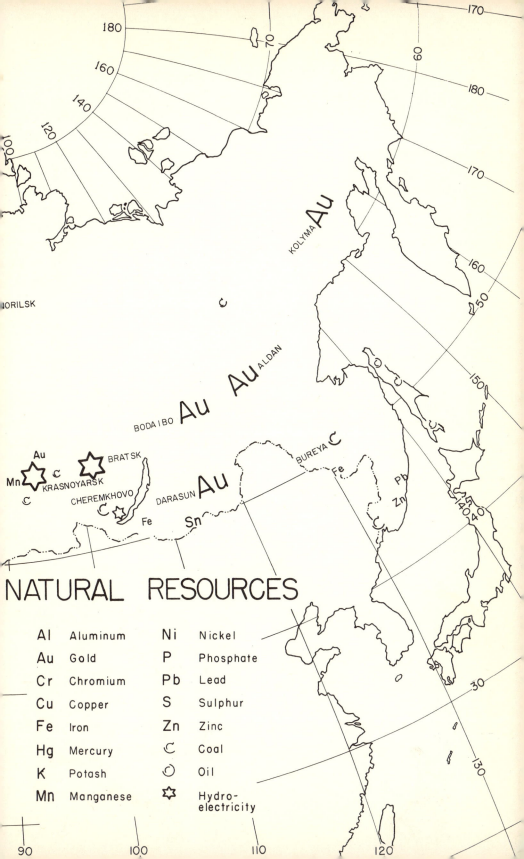

NATURAL RESOURCES

Al	Aluminum	**Ni**	Nickel
Au	Gold	**P**	Phosphate
Cr	Chromium	**Pb**	Lead
Cu	Copper	**S**	Sulphur
Fe	Iron	**Zn**	Zinc
Hg	Mercury	C	Coal
K	Potash	O	Oil
Mn	Manganese	☆	Hydro-electricity

per kilogram.) Coal constitutes by far the largest portion of the fuel
resources of the U.S.S.R. Even considering that the most recent official estimate (1957) indicated that less than 5 per cent of the total
coal may fall in the category of proved reserves, it is believed that
the U.S.S.R. has an almost inexhaustible reserve of this fuel.

In addition to its vast resources of coal, the U.S.S.R. has reserves
of peat and oil shale which can be estimated at roughly 70–80 billion
tons of standard fuel. As in the case of coal, however, the Soviet
Union is still in the process of surveying its raw material resources;
and what the ultimate limits of peat and oil shale may be is unknown.

By the end of the century, significant increases are anticipated in
the proved reserves of both crude petroleum and natural gas—petroleum increasing from an estimated 5.6 billion tons of standard fuel
in 1959 to about 21.5 billion tons in 2000 and natural gas from about
2 billion tons to 24 billion tons in the same period. The data upon
which such estimates are based render invalid any percentage break-
down of these fuels in relation to total primary energy resources.
Since the Soviet Union is planning tremendous expansions in both
petroleum and natural gas production, it is possible that the estimates
of petroleum and natural gas reserves presented in the table represent
minimum rather than maximum resources.

The determination of hydroelectric resources in any country, not
excepting the U.S.S.R., is highly complex, involving among other
factors, determinations about theoretical potential, technical potential, and economic potential. The U.S.S.R. recently reported an annual economic hydroelectric potential, of 137 million kilowatts, and
equated this to 1.2 trillion kilowatt-hours. The accuracy of this
survey and the extent to which physical limiting factors such as
permafrost, ice conditions, and accessibility were considered are
unknown. In terms of theoretical potential, including the flow of
minor rivers, the U.S.S.R. claims to have in excess of 11 percent of
the world's hydroelectric resources. In terms of a more realistic
measure—economic potential—the hydroelectric resources of the
Soviet Union may be about twice those of the United States.

From the nature of developments which have taken place thus far
in the fuels industries of the Soviet Union, problems related to location, topography, climate, and such other natural factors as might
bear on the successful exploitation of primary energy reserves should
be regarded, for the most part, as temporary inconveniences rather
than permanent obstacles. Like their Western contemporaries, the
resource technicians of the U.S.S.R. have demonstrated their com-

petence in overcoming such obstacles. In short, it is believed that there are few of the energy resources which are likely to prove to be out of reach if the planners determine that they are required for successful expansion of industry in the Soviet Union.*

Coal is the great essential of modern industry, for it is the key to power and to many chemical industries. Fortunately its geology is fairly simple so that it is possible to estimate reserves with reasonable accuracy. The Soviet Union holds first or second place among the nations of the world (depending on criteria), with at least three trillion tons and possibly as much as eight trillion tons. The reason for the uncertainty is that some of the estimated reserve is of doubtful quality, but even on a minimum basis there is enough to last for centuries. This is a fabulous resource; its value in rubles or dollars is incalculable. By 1960, the Union was producing about as much as the United States.

Estimates of reserves need interpretation as to quality. Coal may be present in beds a few inches thick, but it does not normally pay to mine seams less than three feet in thickness. Some coal beds lie a mile or two below the surface, but in most cases it is not economically feasible to lift coal more than 3,000 feet. Some coal may contain 50 or 75 per cent ash, but it is normally not worth using when the ash content exceeds 20 per cent. Other mines are so wet that the cost of pumping the water is almost as great as the value of the coal produced. Furthermore, lignite is less valuable than anthracite.

Since uncertainties always exist as to the size of reserves in undeveloped areas, it is customary to divide the total into categories such as valid or proven, probable, and possible. Estimates in the last category include hypothetical assumptions, and, in the case of the Soviet Union, overgenerous criteria. In recent decades, figures for reserves of Soviet coal have risen from 1.6 trillion tons to 8.6 trillion tons, but seven-eighths of the latter is in the "possible" category. In contrast, current American figures are more conservatively compiled, and the totals have been reduced from 3.5 trillion tons to around 2 trillion tons. No other country has as much coal as Russia or the United States, although China may be a close third.

Soviet coal is both abundant and widespread. The Donets field in the Ukraine, north of the Black Sea, leads in production, though not in reserves. It is well to distinguish between buried potentials and actual

* U.S. Congress, Joint Congressional Committee on Atomic Energy, *Background Material for the Review of International Atomic Policies and Programs of the United States*, IV, pp. 1645–46. Washington, D.C. (Oct. 1960).

The Karaganda area ranks third among Soviet coal producers. This is a view of the first fully mechanized shaft. (*Courtesy Soviet Embassy, Washington*)

output, for while the major production is in Europe, the great reserves are in Siberia. In czarist days, the Donets area produced three-quarters of Russia's coal. The fraction has now dropped to one-third, but the total quantity is much larger than before. Donets coal is of high quality; much of it is suitable for making blast furnace coke.

Other important mines in Soviet Europe lie near Moscow, where the coal is mostly lignite; in the Pechora field near the Arctic Circle; on both sides of the Urals, for the most part lignite and sub-bituminous not suitable for metallurgical use; and in the Caucasus. Western Russia is thus well supplied with coal. The chief district without nearby supplies is Leningrad, but the area does have commercial supplies of peat.

At least 90 per cent of all Soviet coal lies east of the Urals. The largest production is in the Kuznetsk Basin of central Siberia, almost unknown under the czar, but now the country's second largest source. The Kuznetsk field has reserves of high grade coal which may total a trillion tons. Here is the equivalent of Pennsylvania, Ohio, West Virginia, and Kentucky all in one. Farther east, around Krasnoyarsk and north along the Tunguska tributaries of the Yenisei, are deposits which may be even larger.

The third producer is Karaganda, north of Lake Balkhash, again a post-revolutionary development. Here some of the coal is near the surface, and is mined with power shovels and shipped to the Urals. Eastern Siberia also has large reserves and a growing production around Lake Baikal, along the Amur River, near Vladivostok, and on Sakhalin Island.

Data on coal reserves in remote areas are obviously more uncertain than those in the developed sections of the country. Along the Lena River, coal is mined in a small way, and the enthusiasm of Soviet writers is shown by one reference to the potentials as "inexhaustible reserves, as yet unexplored."

It is clear that the U.S.S.R. as a whole has vast deposits of coal, and that this coal is widely distributed. Few parts of the country where there is a need for coal are remote from a producing mine, although some of this coal is not of the proper type for metallurgy or other special uses.

Oil is the second great source of power in our modern world. Petroleum is the key to rapid transport on land and by air, to mechanized agriculture, and to a host of chemical operations. Unfortunately, the geology of oil is much more complex than that of coal, so that the extent of the reserves often remains in doubt until all the oil is gone.

It is certain that the Soviet Union has vast amounts of petroleum and natural gas, enough for her present needs and probably enough for some decades to come. On the other hand, the long-range prospects are less attractive than is the case with coal. In any case, the Union is a rapidly growing producer and will probably hold second or third place among the nations of the world for some time to come. By 1960 daily consumption had reached 2,500,000 barrels, and the Union was exporting 500,000 barrels daily.

The petroleum fields around Baku, next to the Caspian in Azerbaidzhan, are among the oldest producing districts on earth, going back about a century. Around 1900 Baku supplied half the world's output, and the district still yields an important share of the Soviet production. Other wells lie to the northwest along the base of the Caucasus Mountains. Between the Urals and the Volga the newly developed reserves appear so tremendous that the Russians term the area a "Second Baku." Other oil fields are present northward to the Arctic. There is also a small production of oil in areas acquired from Poland after the Second World War.

The chief oil production in Siberia is on Sakhalin Island. Most of Soviet Asia appears to be without petroleum, although the sedimentary

The oil fields of the "Second Baku" have become the leading producer in the Soviet Union. This is a view of the Novo Ufimsk refinery in the Ufa area of the Bashkir Autonomous Republic. (*Courtesy Soviet Embassy, Washington*)

basins of Western Siberia may contain oil. Preliminary work in Central Asia, chiefly in the Kazakh-Turkmen area, suggests that it may be rich in oil; it has been termed a "second Middle East."

Most of the Soviet oil reserves are found in a north-south zone from the Caspian to the Arctic, roughly parallel to the Urals. This oil belt is a continuation of the great fields around the Persian Gulf where the Arabian Peninsula, Iran, and Iraq appear to hold the bulk of all the oil on earth.

While Soviet reserves of petroleum are very large, there are elements of weakness in their concentrated location. The production is off-center, so that long hauls are necessary to supply many areas. Much oil still moves by railroad tank car or river barge.

Natural gas has become a significant industrial fuel, with large fields in Middle Asia around Tashkent, the lower Ob, the Caucasus, and the Ukraine.

One of the most important postwar fuel developments was the construction of thousands of miles of pipe lines for oil and gas. These lead from the producing fields to the major cities, including points as far west as Odessa, Kiev, Minsk, and Leningrad, as well as east to Tashkent and Irkutsk. As a result, the industrial areas of the Ukraine, Moscow, and the Urals now have a new source of cheap fuel. One of the world's largest pipe lines carries oil to central Europe.

Uranium and thorium deposits are known to occur widely, but only limited information is available as to production or reserves for atomic energy. Several references mention deposits in the Fergana Valley of Middle Asia, the Kara Tau Mountains, the Urals, Krivoi Rog, and Estonia. Other areas with suitable geology for occurences include Karelia and the Kola Peninsula, the Ukrainian Shield area, the northern Caucasus-Aral Sea area, the Altai-Sayan Mountains, Trans-Baikalia, the Aldan region, and the Soviet Far East. Production in the European satellites may be larger than in the Union itself. The accompanying table of uranium reserves suggests that the U.S.S.R. does not have outstanding resources.

URANIUM RESERVES*

(Short Tons of U_3O_8)†

Canada	400,000
South Africa	370,000
United States	250,000
Soviet bloc	120–450,000
World Total	1,190,000–1,520,000

* U.S. Congress, Joint Congressional Committee on Atomic Energy, *Review of the International Atomic Policies and Programs of the United States*, 1, p. 38. Washington, D.C. (Oct. 1960).

† Based on production costs of $10 per pound.

Materials for Construction

Iron is the great metal, indispensable for construction purposes and valuable for its magnetic properties in generating electricity. Here again the Soviet Union is most fortunate, for iron ore is abundant. Enormous claims are made for potential reserves, but the deposits actually measured are more limited although still adequate for many decades.

Half the iron ore of the Soviet Union lies in or near the Ukraine. The central Ukraine has ore similar to that near Lake Superior, and is the greatest producing center. Very large reserves also lie in or near the Urals, which is second in output. This includes Magnitogorsk and

The Novo Lipetsk blast furnaces operate on iron ore from the open cut mines at Kursk. This is a fully integrated plant with a coke-chemical complex, electric furnaces, and continuous strip rolling mills. (*Courtesy Soviet Embassy, Washington*)

the new developments at Kachkanarsk and Kustani. The remainder of the reserves, largely undeveloped, is made up of deposits near Moscow, along the Volga, around Lake Baikal, and in the Far East. Scattered deposits occur elsewhere, but the over-all picture is far more concentrated than with coal.

The Ukraine is the leading metallurgical center, for the iron ore of Krivoi Rog is only 200 miles west of Donets coking coal. Midway

The Kursk Magnetic Anomaly contains one of the largest deposits of iron ore on earth. This excavator has a capacity of removing 500 cubic meters of overburden per hour. (*Courtesy Soviet Embassy, Washington*)

between them is the Dnieper River with its electricity for making alloy steels and chemicals. Here is the Union's number one center of heavy industry, and one of the great steel areas of the world. Unfortunately for the Russians, this area was overrun by the Germans during both world wars.

In addition to the iron ore at Krivoi Rog, very large reserves are present at Kerch in the Crimea and at Kursk, where a magnetic anomaly has long been recognized.

The Ukraine is the leading industrial republic of the Union, and its coal and steel form the base for great factories such as those around Kharkov where tractors, farm implements, locomotives, machine tools, and electrical goods are produced in increasing volume. Single factories employing 20,000 people are common.

Whereas the Ukraine once dominated Soviet industry, developments in the Urals are now a close second. The Urals contain great amounts of iron ore, but unfortunately the only near-by coal is of inferior quality, ill suited for use in a blast furnace. Suitable coking coal is present at Karaganda and at Kuznetsk in central Siberia, but each is hundreds of miles away. The early Five Year Plans developed a Ural-Kuznetsk combine, despite the cost of the 1,200-mile haul, with giant blast furnaces at both ends of the line.

The Altyn-Topkan lead-zinc mine in southeastern Uzbekistan transports its ore from the mine to the dressing plant by a cableway. The elevation exceeds 6,000 feet. (*Courtesy Soviet Embassy, Washington*)

Unlike the United States, which has the Great Lakes as a highway for moving the ore of Minnesota to the coal of Pennsylvania, no waterways link Soviet iron and coal. Nowhere in the capitalist world does it pay to haul coal or iron ore long distances by rail, but under socialist bookkeeping the extra expense is passed on to other sectors of the economy.

Great steel works, as at Magnitogorsk, have transformed sleepy villages into large factory towns. Iron production in the Urals goes back to the days of Peter the Great, when shipments were even made to England. From the great tonnages of Ural steel come tractors made at Chelyabinsk; railroad equipment from Nizhni Tagil; heavy machinery at Sverdlovsk; and military supplies from unspecified places. One may fly across the Soviet Union for many miles and see only field and forest, or desert and tundra, but it is the booming industrial development in these mining and manufacturing centers which makes possible the changing Soviet economy.

Modern industry calls for copper, lead, zinc, aluminum, a long list of alloys, and a growing array of accessory metals. For most of these the U.S.S.R. has a good supply. The United States has little or no tin, nickel, manganese, asbestos, chromium, platinum, or antimony, all of which are present in the Soviet Union.

Aluminum is one of man's most useful metals, but was not produced in the Soviet Union until 1932. While present in all clays, the usual raw material is bauxite, which is relatively uncommon. The Soviet Union has considerable reserves of bauxite, but its aluminum production is supplemented from other aluminum-bearing minerals such as alunite, silimanite, and nepheline. Early developments near Leningrad and Zaporozhe (on the Dnieper) have been surpassed by operations in the Urals, Stalingrad, and central Siberia. New plants at Pavlodar, Krasnoyarsk, and Irkutsk are expected to produce a million tons a year by 1965, roughly 70 per cent of the national total. Former shortages should then be cared for.

Soviet copper production illustrates a situation which is common to several minerals. Between 1925 and 1960, the output increased from 10,000 to over 600,000 tons. This is an amazing expansion, but was barely enough to meet the needs. Domestic copper has been chronically in short supply, with imports whenever possible. The Urals have reserves of fair quality ore but the amount is far from adequate. Large deposits have been developed near Lake Balkhash and elsewhere in Middle Asia, but the complex mineralogy and low percentage of metal makes refining expensive. Elsewhere in the world, commercal deposits of copper ore carry 1 or 2 per cent metallic copper. Many Soviet deposits are much leaner, some of them down to one-half of 1 per cent metal. The copper is present, but the cost of extraction may become too high.

It is well to remember that the term "ore" has an economic rather than a geological definition. Metal may be present in a rock, but if it cannot be extracted at a profit, the rock is not an ore. One of the unique aspects of socialist economy is that it does not ask, "Will it pay?" but rather, "Is it desirable?" If national welfare calls for a certain development, costs are secondary.

Lead supplies are quite deficient; sulphur presents another serious shortage.

Gold is superabundant, and Soviet production may rank next to South Africa, which leads the world. Great amounts are obtained from placer operations along the Yenisei, Lena, and Kolyma rivers. The production is uncertain but appears to exceed five million ounces a

The Azovstal steel mill in the southern Ukraine lies on the shores of the Sea of Azov midway between Donets coal and Kerch iron ore. (*Courtesy Soviet Embassy, Washington*)

year, worth 35 dollars an ounce. Much of the gold dug out of the ground in Siberia is sold on the world market in London, and finds its way back into the ground at Fort Knox.

In her reserves of platinum, asbestos, potash, phosphate rock, chromium, and manganese, the Soviet Union takes high rank and has a surplus for export. Diamonds are mined in Yakutia.

Potentials for Industry

The over-all Soviet mineral picture is mixed. It is clear that the nation has very great reserves, but one should not confuse deeply buried deposits of complex minerals, remote from coal or other power, and far from markets, with refined metals ready for industry. Nevertheless, here are the makings of a great industrial nation. No wonder the Soviet people have a patriotic thrill in their fatherland, and no wonder the Soviet government takes a strong political position in international affairs.

The Soviet Union is more nearly self-sufficient than any other nation. The country would doubtless like to have international trade, but it can get along without imports if necessary. A complete economic blockade would pinch, but not seriously.

Three centers of heavy industry stand out, each based on near-by mines. The central Ukraine leads by far, thanks to coal in the Donets Basin, iron from Krivoi Rog, high grade manganese and other local raw materials, plus hydroelectric power on the Dnieper. Although Kharkov lies to one side of the mineralized area, its metal fabricating industries are parasitic on the near-by centers of primary production.

The Urals are a great storehouse of minerals, in some respects the richest and certainly the most diversified area in the Union. Suitable coal must be brought from a distance, but petroleum and natural gas are near by. Iron ore is very abundant, and along with it copper, aluminum, chromium, manganese, and many other minerals. As a result, cities such as Sverdlovsk have become great manufacturing centers.

The third industrial center focuses on the Kuznetsk Basin in central Siberia, famous for its coal. Modest amounts of iron, manganese, lead, zinc, and other metals lie near by. Novosibirsk is an industrial beneficiary in the same way that Kharkov profits from Donets primary production.

Looking ahead, one may anticipate important industrial developments along the Angara and upper Yenisei rivers when their vast hydropower is developed. Coal, iron, and aluminum are also available, so that the Krasnoyarsk-Irkutsk area may become very significant.

Chapter V

RIVER DEVELOPMENTS

BOTH THE history and the geography of Russia might be written in terms of its rivers. Centuries ago they served as avenues for the exploration of the east; today they carry large amounts of freight and are an important source of electricity. Except where rivers flow through mountainous areas, gradients are generally low enough for navigation. More than eighty thousand miles of waterways are in use, although some are employed only for rafting timber.

River Problems

Unfortunately, most Soviet rivers flow in the wrong direction. The great Siberian rivers, the Ob, Yenisei, and Lena, end in the Arctic Sea, which is frozen for nine or ten months a year. The Amur heads for the Pacific but turns northward along its last 500 miles and has an estuary which is shallow and icebound for many months. The south-flowing Volga is by far the most important river, carrying over half the inland waterborne commerce, but it ends in the landlocked Caspian. The Don and Dnieper reach the Black Sea, but the Black Sea is bottled up by the Bosporus. Nowhere does a Soviet river provide free access to the open ocean.

The Moscow–Volga Canal enables the capital to advertise itself as the "Port of the Five Seas," with access northward to the Baltic and White seas and south to the Caspian, Azov, and Black seas. The locks are large enough to accommodate seagoing vessels. (*Sovfoto*)

85

How different Russia's economy and outlook might have been if she had had a navigable river which reached the high seas—if there had been, for example, a Mississippi flowing south to the Indian Ocean, or a Great Lakes-St. Lawrence system entering the Pacific at Vladivostok, or a Columbia River joining the Atlantic at a Soviet Portland. One of the key words in Soviet geography is continentality, and one of the reasons for the absence of maritime orientation lies in the lack of free access to the open ocean.

The major orientation of travel across Siberia has always been west-east, at right angles to the flow of the rivers. Early travelers crossed to the Pacific by a combination of travel by boat and short overland portages. From the Volga system it is possible to go up a tributary of the Kama to a point on the eastern side of the Urals. From the head of navigation in the Kama basin, it is only a few miles to an east-flowing tributary of the Tobol which, in turn, joins the Irtysh and the Ob.

Farther east, Ob tributaries rise near the Yenisei, and a small canal links the two systems. Travelers then proceed up the Angara to Lake Baikal. No low-level divide leads from the Angara to the Lena, but the distance is short. If bound for the Amur, the traveler may go overland 250 miles from Ulan Ude on the Selenga to Chita on an Amur tributary and thence float downriver to the Pacific. Where travel follows down the Lena and continues up the Aldan, the destination is the Sea of Okhotsk. By the use of this west-to-east route, Russian explorers reached the Pacific in 1639, only six decades after Yermak crossed the Urals and began the conquest of Siberia.

Soviet rivers are widely spaced. Few parts of the Soviet Union receive as much rainfall as the United States, so that her runoff per square mile is less. Over large sections the average precipitation is only half that of the area east of the Mississippi. The deserts of Soviet Middle Asia are drier than the American Great Basin, and her highlands are so far from the ocean that they receive less snow than most mountains in the United States.

As a result of the high latitudes and long winters, most rivers are frozen for six months, and the ice may be four feet thick. Even in the southern part of Soviet Europe rivers may be blocked by ice during four months. Where streams flow northwards, ice melts along their headwaters and spring floods develop upstream while the lower course is still dammed by ice. Spring thaw begins in southern Siberia in mid-April, but does not start in the Arctic until June; spring floods thus reach the north before spring temperatures have started to thaw the river ice. Due to this climatic background, Soviet rivers vary widely in their seasonal flow, being lowest in winter and reaching a brief but intense flood with the melting of the snow and surface permafrost.

In order to modify the limitations of the river pattern, canals link several systems. Some of these are small canals which date back for a century, while others are modern and capable of carrying large river steamers. Among the more important are those which join the Volga with its neighbors to the north and west.

WATER UTILIZATION*

	1913	1958	1965 Plan
Inland waterways (miles)	40,050	82,708	94,000
Canals (miles)	1,922	6,000	9,360
Water freight (million tons)	35,100	177,400	265,000
Irrigated land (million acres)	8,650,000	17,785,000	26,180,000
Hydroelectric power (billion kilowatts)	0.04	46.5	100

* Vendrov, S. L. and Kalinin, G. P., "Surface-Water Resources of the U.S.S.R.: Their Utilization and Study," *Soviet Geography*, I, No. 6, pp. 35–49 (1960).

Because of the unequal distribution of moisture, 10 per cent of the Union is too wet and requires drainage, while 40 per cent is too dry and needs irrigation. These figures exclude the tundra, where cultivation is out of the question. This is one of the reasons why plans are proposed for diverting water from one drainage basin to another, such as from the Pechora south to the Volga, or from the Irtysh into Kazakhstan.

Although Soviet inland waterways are extensive, and their tonnage is increasing, they handle but 5 per cent of the nation's total freight turnover. The United States, with only one-quarter of the mileage, moves five times as many ton miles by water. Bulk commodities represent the chief freight, with lumber accounting for about half the tonnage. Oil, coal, grain, and construction materials account for 5 to 10 per cent each. River traffic in petroleum is diminishing with the availability of pipe lines. Where north-south movement is involved, some of the traffic involves the exchange of products from the various climatic zones, such as wood moving south from the taiga, or grain and animal products shipped north from the steppe.

All but one of the country's major seaports lie near the mouth of a river. The exception is Vladivostok. Along the Black Sea the principal ports are Odessa and Rostov-on-Don. On the Baltic, Russia's gateways are Leningrad and Riga. Each of the Arctic rivers has its port: Arkhangelsk on the Northern Dvina, Salekhard on the Ob, Igarka on the Yenisei, and Tiksi on the Lena. The important thing about Soviet seaports is that, with one or two exceptions, the cities are relatively unimportant. Not even Leningrad rates among the fifty leading seaports of the world, and only two or three ports have regular sailings of foreign passenger vessels.

In order to increase the flow of the Volga and thus provide water for irrigation and power, and to insure enough water at the mouth of the Volga so that the level of the Caspian Sea will not drop, it is proposed to dam the north-flowing Pechora and divert some of its water southward through the low divide into the Volga basin.

Irrigation has long been practiced, especially in the drier lands of Middle Asia and the Ukraine. Cotton is the principal irrigated field crop, followed by rice, sugar beets, alfalfa, tobacco, fruits and vegetables. Some developments lie near the base of snow-covered mountains, as in the Caucasus or the Pamirs; other areas are along the lower course of rivers such as the Don and Volga which pass from humid into drier lands. The ambitious character of the over-all irrigation program is obvious when the area of the new storage lakes is examined. By the end of 1965, the total reservoir area throughout the Union will exceed twelve million acres. Some conception of the extent of these artificial lakes is assisted by considering that their shore lines will exceed the combined length of the coasts of the Soviet inland seas. The total area of these reservoirs is such that evaporation from their surfaces will result in considerable losses.

These reservoirs will irrigate several tens of millions of acres, but this must be balanced against fertile flood plains submerged and taken out of cultivation. It has been necessary to move many towns, and to construct new communication facilities. Numerous historic river ports are now beneath the water. Boats which once were suitable for small rivers are now too small for reservoirs several miles wide. For example, the Tsimlyanskaya reservoir sometimes has ten-foot waves; small wonder that the Russians call it a "sea."

Reservoirs tend to reduce the hazard of spring floods, and their storage capacity reduces the problem of occasional drought. If the objective is to generate electricity or supply water for irrigation, the water level should be maintained at the highest possible level, but if flood control is desired, reservoirs should be kept partially empty.

Engineers may alter the face of the earth, but when man changes the balance of nature he must consider the consequences. The introduction of irrigation water onto desert fields often results in waterlogging large areas with gentle slopes, or in the concentration of soluble salts. Whether irrigation benefits outweigh the undesirable effects remains to be seen.

One of the most ambitious projects, still highly tentative, looks forward to the creation of a "Central Siberian Sea" to cover nearly 400,000 square miles of the middle valley of the Ob and reach, irregularly, from the Urals to Lake Baikal. An area to the south, of similar size, would then be provided with irrigation.

Hydroelectricity

Early in the series of Five Year Plans the Soviets decided on large-scale development of their hydroelectric potential. This was in part a reflection of Lenin's belief that electricity is the key to industrialization. The dam on the Dnieper was the third biggest hydropower producer

The Angara River has a relatively constant volume since it flows out of Lake Baikal. This is the site of the great Bratsk dam; when built, it was the largest single source of hydroelectricity on earth. (*Courtesy Soviet Embassy, Washington*)

in the world when built. Still bigger dams have been completed at Kuibyshev and Volgagrad (Stalingrad) on the Volga, and at Bratsk on the Angara, each the largest in the world when constructed. Even more impressive developments are under way, with surveys which call for very large amounts of hydroelectricity.

There is no question as to the capacity of the Soviet Union to build huge dams and generators, or of the great over-all potential, but the country faces environmental limitations. Hydropower has two basic requirements: dependable year-round runoff and steep gradients. Rainfall in much of the Soviet Union is only twenty inches, roughly half that of the eastern United States, and precipitation varies considerably from season to season, and from year to year. Thick ice presents further flow problems. Much of the inhabited parts of the country, where there is a need for electricity, is so flat that rivers have low gradients; suitable dam sites are few, or else structures must be miles in length. Large reservoir capacity may be needed to balance flood flow against low water stages of the river.

While the U.S.S.R. accounts for 16 per cent of the world's land area outside Antarctica, its relatively low rainfall means that it has only 13 per cent of the world's stream flow. This runoff, coupled with gentle gradients, provides for only 11 per cent of the world's theoretical water power potential.

A river should be more than an avenue for discharging surplus rainfall. Under Soviet planning, each river is to be managed so that it renders its maximum service from source to mouth, with priorities assigned to hydroelectric power, navigation, irrigation, flood control, fish and recreation, and domestic and industrial water, in that order.

The process by which this multi-purpose full-development objective is to be achieved is through the construction of an integrated series of dams. Each major river will be converted into a staircase, with a succession of power dams and long reservoirs. Both cascades and shoals will disappear, and flood peaks as well. Ideally, the river will almost cease to have a current and the operation of gravity will be concentrated at the dam sites. Such integrated programs were first developed by the Tennessee Valley Authority, and are in process of realization along the Volga.

The over-all hydroelectric potential of the Soviet Union is estimated to be 420,000,000 kilowatts, less than a tenth of which has been developed. The bulk of this somewhat hypothetical resource lies in eastern Siberia, far from present needs. In terms of the principal river basins, current development programs expressed in million kilowatts are as follows: Yenisei—28 (of which 10 are along the Angara), Lena—18, Amur—6, Indigirka—6, Volga—6, Naryn—6, Ab-i-Panj (Pamirs)—6, and Ob—6. Stated in per capita terms, the people of the Tadzhik republic have a possible 8.8 kilowatt-hours per person while in the Ukraine the figure is 0.07.

Plans call for dozens of great dams, on dozens of rivers. Over a hundred hydroelectric plants are in operation, and during the Seven Year Plan their capacity was to increase from 10,500,000 kilowatts in 1958 to 23,000,000 kilowatts in 1965. In comparison, thermal electric capacity was to increase from 42,000,000 to 90,000,000 kilowatts in the same period. In order to place the U.S.S.R. in its proper setting with the U.S.A., the latter's installed capacity in 1959 totaled 31,788,000 kilowatts of hydroelectric power and 143,210,000 kilowatts of thermal electricity. In per capita terms, the United States had an annual per capita

The Gyumush hydroelectric station is one of several power plants along the river which flows out of Lake Sevan in the Armenian Republic. This plant operates on a thousand-foot head, and was completed in 1953. (*Courtesy Soviet Embassy, Washington*)

capacity of 4,490 kilowatt-hours in 1959, as compared with 1,183 in the Soviet Union.

Despite spectacular progress in the hydroelectric field, water power accounts for only one-quarter of Soviet electrical energy. Thermal electricity generated from coal, gas, oil, and peat, will apparently continue to lead indefinitely. The atomic power capacity in 1962 amounted to only 515,000 kilowatts.

The two largest dams on the Volga are at Kuibyshev and Volgagrad, each with a capacity in excess of 2,000,000 kilowatts. Some of the power is used in nearby industry and railways, some is used to pump water for irrigation, and some is sent 500 miles to Moscow. The Kuibyshev Reservoir extends 400 miles upstream, while that above Volgagrad measures 370 miles. Although these artificial lakes are narrow, they

The Lenin power station at Volgagrad has a capacity of 2,530,000 kilowatts, the largest source of hydroelectricity along the Volga cascade. Some of the energy is sent as far as Moscow. (*Courtesy U.S.S.R. National Committee, I.G.U.*)

inundate over two million acres, much of it formerly good agricultural land. Five other dams on the Volga and the Kama are eventually to generate a million kilowatts or more.

Very great amounts of electricity are available along the upper Yenisei and Angara rivers, so that the Krasnoyarsk-Irkutsk area may look forward to major industrialization. In fact, the eventual development of Siberia's hydroelectric potential may reshape the industrial map of the nation.

Around the world at the beginning of 1960 there were only a dozen hydroelectric plants installed or under construction with a capacity of at least a million kilowatts, about evenly divided between the United States and the Soviet Union.

Not only have the Soviets built the world's largest dams and hydroelectric stations, with the largest generators, but they have the world's longest transmission lines. The first Seven Year Plan involved five integrated power grids: the Europe-Urals, Central Asia, Central Siberia, Trans-Caucasus, and Northwest networks. An Eastern Siberia grid is to be added later, so that surplus power may be moved from coast to coast.

River Systems

The Volga is Russia's Main Street, and in its basin live sixty million people. When the dam system is complete there will be a ten-foot waterway for 2,000 miles. Chief among the eastern tributaries is the Kama, which comes out of the Urals, and is navigable for 1,000 miles. From the west the Volga receives the Oka, whose most useful tributary is the Moscow River. The Volga is the largest and longest river in western Eurasia, with a length of 2,325 miles and a drainage area of 563,300 square miles. Its source lies in the Valdai Hills at an elevation of only 665 feet, and where it enters the Caspian Sea the elevation is 85 feet below sea level.

The navigation period at Yaroslavl, north of Moscow, lasts from 170 to 215 days, while Astrakhan near the mouth is ice-free from 225 to 330 days.

Regular boat service on the Oka River links Moscow with Gorki, five days downstream, and from there one may travel on Volga boats to Astrakhan, six days to the south. The Volga System carries one-half the passenger traffic on the inland waterways of the Union, and handles two-thirds of the freight.

Moscow-Astrakhan Boat Service

Downstream (read down)				Upstream (read up)	
Day	Hour	Miles		Hour	Day
		Oka River Boats			
1	16:00	0	Moscow	5:15	6
2	11:05	109	Kolomna	8:35	5
2	23:15	213	Ryazan	15:35	4
4	16:05	528	Murom	13:45	2
5	11:55	661	Gorki	16:00	1
		Volga River Boats			
1	21:00	0	Gorki	14:00	10
2	14:20	267	Kazan	15:35	8
3	13:00	535	Kuibyshev	7:55	6
4	10:30	826	Saratov	8:20	4
5	6:15	1,086	Volgagrad	5:35	2
6	5:00	1,393	Astrakhan	10:00	1

The lower Volga valley is a grassland, fertile but too dry for dependable agriculture. One of the major objectives of the hydroelectric program is to pump water onto the trans-Volga steppe. The program is somewhat similar to that near the Columbia River south of Grand Coulee. More than two million acres are involved; in fact, it is hoped someday to irrigate as much as ten million acres with water, but such a program is for the distant future. It must also be recognized that the flow of the river fluctuates widely from year to year; there will surely be times when there is not enough water to supply the demand if plans are overambitious.

Most of the water to be used for irrigation along the Volga will be withdrawn from the Kuibyshev and Volgagrad reservoirs and pumped into main canals more or less parallel to the river. Another project looks forward to a canal which will link the Volga with the Ural River. This would extend 365 miles east from Volgagrad across semidesert country. The Ural is nearly dry in summer and at times no water reaches the Caspian Sea.

Several canals join the Volga with neighboring rivers. The headwaters of the Volga have long been linked with streams which lead to Lake Onega and Lake Ladoga, and thence to Leningrad and the Baltic. This Mariinsk Canal system dates from 1808, and has been enlarged so that it can handle seagoing vessels with a draft of 12 feet and up to

3,000 tons. Along with the Mariinsk Canal plans, the upper Volga is to be dredged and improved where necessary. Long stretches will be transformed into a chain of navigable reservoirs by new dams.

Near the capital is the 75-mile Moscow-Volga Canal, with locks 18 feet deep. Through the latter, Moscow now has access to the White, Baltic, Caspian, Azov, and Black seas. The city has thus achieved its goal of becoming a "Port of the Five Seas."

At Volgagrad the course of the Volga comes within 48 miles of that of the Don, to which it was joined by a canal and 13 locks in 1952. Since the canal follows an irregular course, its length is 62 miles. At this point the Volga is 75 feet below sea level while the divide between the rivers is 220 feet above the sea, and the Don in turn lies at an elevation of 70 feet. Each lock is 500 feet long, 60 feet wide, and has a depth of 13 feet. In order to generate electricity with which to pump water

The Volga is Russia's "Main Street," carrying more ships and barges than any other Soviet river. This view, near the mouth, shows the port of Astrakhan. (*Courtesy Soviet Embassy, Washington*)

to the upper part of the Volga-Don Canal, a dam blocks the Don at Tsimlyanskaya.

Through the Volga-Don Canal, coal and iron from the Ukraine may move by barge into the Caspian area, while oil from the Volga fields may be shipped to the west. Grain, lumber, ores, and manufactured goods add to the traffic. Unfortunately, the canal is closed by ice during four or five months each year.

In a special sense, these waterways make Western Europe an island rather than a peninsula. The combination of these waterways enables the Union to move small merchant ships and naval vessels between Arctic, Baltic, and Black sea areas along interior lines.

The Volga's relation to the Caspian problem has long concerned Soviet scientists. The level of the sea fluctuates with the shifting balance between supply and evaporation. In recent decades there has been a steady drop in level, and when the Volga's reservoirs and irrigation schemes are in operation the discharge of the Volga may diminish by a fifth. For several years, the water at the port of Baku has become progressively more shallow. This was especially serious when Baku shipped the bulk of the nation's oil; now that the output of near-by wells is declining and petroleum is available elsewhere, Caspian navigation has become less significant.

Four navigable rivers flow south to the Black Sea, the Don in the east, the Dnieper in the center, and the Bug and the Dniester to the west. All of these rivers, along with tributaries such as the Donets, have a strikingly parallel course as they flow to the southeast. This alignment matches the geologic structure, for the streams follow the base of low escarpments formed by sediments which dip gently to the southwest. Where the rivers turn to cross these hard rocks there are rapids.

The Don has a length of 1,325 miles, and drains 166,000 square miles of low, rolling country. Water from the Tsimlyanskaya reservoir, near the Volga-Don Canal, will be used to irrigate two million acres of semi-arid steppe, one-third by gravity flow and the rest by pumping. This gain in cropland must be placed against the half million acres inundated by the reservoir, much of it good flood-plain soil.

The Don receives tributaries which come from the Caucasus as well as those which flow out of central Russia. Because of this, there are two annual flood periods. One, known as the cold water flood, is caused by the melting of snow in the mountains, while the other, or warm water flood, stems from spring thaw in the northern part of the basin. Near its mouth, the Don is closed by ice for 125 days a year.

The Dnieper is a major river, with a length of 1,410 miles and a drainage basin of 202,140 square miles, five times the area of New York State. The river rises in the Pripet Marshes, where old canals lead to the Baltic and westward into Poland. Below Kiev, 660 miles from the Black Sea, the Dnieper is navigable for vessels drawing 10 feet. Where the river crosses a spur of the Carpathians and turns to the southwest there is a series of rapids with a drop of 155 feet.

Proposals to improve navigation around the rapids date from 1732, but the problem was not solved until the construction of the country's first great dam, at Zaporozhe in 1932. When built, this supplied the third largest hydrostation in the world, with a capacity of 650,000 kilowatts. Additional dams are planned, and the Zaporozhe capacity is to be increased so that the Dnieper system will have an output of over two million kilowatts. The availability of this electric power halfway between the coal of the Donets Basin and the iron ore of Krivoi Rog has given rise to electrochemical industries and the manufacture of alloy steels.

The Dniester enters the sea near Odessa, Russia's main port on the Black Sea, but the river is of limited value for navigation. As with the Don, there are two flood periods: that in February and March caused by the break-up of the ice, and the other in June due to melting snow in the Carpathians. As a reminder of the high latitudes, Odessa, even though it is in the southern part of the Union, occupies a position analogous to that of Duluth on Lake Superior.

The southern Ukraine is marginally dry and has often been a famine land. Elaborate canal systems divert water from the Dnieper and will eventually irrigate three million acres. In addition, water is to be supplied to the northern and eastern Crimea, where an additional two million acres need water. Far-reaching projects announced during the 1950's called for the irrigation of many million acres in the arid and semi-arid lands of the lower Dnieper, Don, and Volga. A decade later it appeared that most of these goals would not be realized for many years.

When the irrigation programs along the Don and the Dnieper are completed, the rivers will contribute less water to the Black Sea. This may lower the level of the sea and even reverse the currents through the Bosporus.

Two rivers flow to the Baltic Sea: the Western Dvina, whose mouth is at Riga, and the short Neva, on whose delta lies the city of Leningrad. Neither is important in itself, but the Neva forms the outlet for lakes Ladoga and Onega, and these in turn provide access to the White

Every river which flows through the taiga carries its load of logs to the nearest pulp or saw mill. This view is in the Krasnoyarsk Kray. (*Courtesy U.S.S.R. National Committee, I.G.U.*)

Sea and the Mariinsk Canals. The White Sea Canal, built during the early Five Year Plans, can carry vessels of up to 1,250 tons.

The European part of the Soviet Arctic also receives two rivers, both of them of considerable size. The Northern Dvina, whose delta is the site for Arkhangelsk, drains 141,000 square miles of forest country and has a length, counting the main tributary, of 1,350 miles. A 45-mile canal leads to the upper Volga, but the locks are small. The Northern Dvina is ice-blocked for 190 days a year; during the open period it is extensively used for rafting timber, so that Arkhangelsk is the country's main lumber port.

Farther east is the Pechora River, 1,150 miles long. Ten-foot depths are available for 580 miles, as compared with 400 miles on the Northern Dvina. Much of the Pechora basin is undeveloped, but large deposits of coal and oil point to an important future.

In the heart of arid Soviet Middle Asia lies the shallow Aral Sea, fourth largest inland water body on earth. Two streams bring water from the snow-crowned Pamirs, the Amu Darya and the Syr Darya. Both grow progressively smaller as they cross the desert, for they lose water by evaporation, seepage, and diversion for oasis irrigation. Both exceed 1,000 miles in length, and both have reservoirs and power projects in their headwaters and irrigation projects where they leave the mountains.

It is proposed to link the Amu Darya with the Caspian Sea across Turkmenia, a distance of 680 miles. During the moister climate of Pleistocene times, the Aral Sea, terminus of the Amu Darya, filled its basin to overflowing and a fresh-water lake drained westward to the

Hundreds of canals bring water to the dry areas of Soviet Middle Asia. This is a view of the Kara Kum Canal in the Turkmenian Republic. (*Courtesy U.S.S.R. National Committee, I.G.U.*)

Caspian, which in turn overflowed to the Black Sea. The Turkmenian Canal is designed primarily to provide irrigation in the intervening desert, since power and navigation possibilities are negligible. The area scheduled for cultivation exceeds three million acres, but some of the soils have saline or alkaline characteristics. Any water supply from the Amu Darya which reaches the end of the canal will help to maintain the level of the Caspian. The Aral Sea, in turn, will shrink.

Four great Siberian rivers are among the dozen longest on earth: the Ob, Yenisei, Lena, and Amur. Each has major tributaries over a thousand miles long which are great rivers in their own right: respectively, the Irtysh, the Angara, the Aldan, and the Sungari. Vast hydroelectric potentials await development along all of the above.

The Ob rises in the Altai Mountains and flows 3,200 miles to the Arctic Ocean after draining over a million square miles. Its major tributary, the Irtysh, has a length of 2,700 miles. Below their junction lie the great Vasyugan swamps, accessible only when frozen. Upstream on both rivers are vast wheatlands, farther south is the dry steppe, while humid mountains lie near their source. So great is the volume of these rivers that the Ob is navigable for ships drawing ten feet of water for 1,700 miles, while the Irtysh has 450 miles similarly accessible.

Hydroelectric potentials in the Ob basin are limited to the headwaters, for farther downstream gradients amount to only a few inches per mile and the banks are so low that dams would have to be miles in length. Nine projects are planned for the upper Ob, with a total capacity of 12,000,000 kilowatts, while plans for its tributary, the Irtysh, look forward to 16 dams. Several installations of half a million kilowatts are already in operation on both rivers, including a dam near Novosibirsk.

The Yenisei is the Union's longest river, with a length of 3,553 miles, a drainage basin of over a million square miles, and an average discharge of 600,000 cubic feet per second. Where crossed by the Trans-Siberian Railway at Krasnoyarsk the river is 4,000 feet wide, while at the seaport of Igarka, 450 miles from the ocean, the width is four miles. The middle course is icebound for 180 days, and the river is frozen for 235 days near the mouth; when it is open, 225-foot boats easily reach points south of Minusinsk, 1,852 miles from the mouth.

No less than 20 hydroelectric plants are planned for the Yenisei and its tributaries, with a total capacity of 20,000,000 kilowatts. Above the city of Krasnoyarsk a 5,000,000-kilowatt power plant is in construction. The dam is 330 feet high and forms a reservoir 250 miles long. Downstream a 6,000,000-kilowatt installation is projected.

Equally large developments lie along the Angara, a 1,200-mile tributary which has a nearly constant volume since it flows out of Lake Baikal; the river has a drop of 1,180 feet between the lake and its junction with the Yenisei. Six dams are projected, of which those at Irkutsk and Bratsk have been completed. The latter, with an installed capacity of 4,500,000 kilowatts, was the world's largest power plant when built.

The Lena and the Amur also hold major power potentials, but they are so remote from present needs that only limited hydroelectric developments are in sight. One plan calls for the joint development of power along the Middle Amur where it forms the international boundary with China. Both rivers carry large steamers during the six months when they are open for navigation. The Lena is economically the least developed of Russia's major rivers since it was not reached by railway until after the Second World War.

Large canals link several Soviet rivers. This is a view of the entrance to the Volga-Don Canal. (*Courtesy U.S.S.R. National Committee, I.G.U.*)

Chapter VI

SOVIET EUROPE

VARIOUS REGIONAL schemes have been proposed for the Soviet Union, some purely in physical terms, others largely cultural. One of the simplest schemes of regionalization is through natural vegetation, which in turn represents broad climatic zones. Tundra, taiga, steppe, desert, and the miscellaneous mountain landscapes form a basic framework. Other regional divisions may emphasize landforms, or soils, or geologic structure, or nationalities. Since Soviet planning is directed toward agricultural and industrial potentials, many Russian studies seek to define economic regions. Political areas seldom form satisfactory units for geographic analysis.

The regions here described may be termed *geographic*, in that they seek to describe over-all unity, with a blending of physical and cultural components. No area, not even a single square foot, has complete unity; all that classification can attempt is to define an area within which there is an essential coherence and which differs from adjoining areas in some significant feature.

Within the Soviet realm as a whole are 3 major geographic provinces and 25 regions: Soviet Europe, with 10 regions; Middle Asia, with 5 regions; and Siberia, with 10 geographic regions.

Several colleges of the University of Moscow are housed in the central part of this 31-story building on the Lenin Hills in the southern part of the city. The Department of Geography has six of the upper floors, with a comprehensive regional museum in the tower. Faculty apartments and student dormitories occupy the wings. (*Courtesy Soviet Embassy, Washington*)

It is obvious that the wheatfields and giant industries of the Ukraine have little similarity to the empty deserts of Turkmenia or the trackless forests of the Yakut Republic. Metropolitan Moscow has no more in common with tiny Siberian villages than New York City resembles a Wyoming ranch. No casual traveler should expect to see all of the U.S.S.R., and no reader of this volume should expect to understand the complexities of the several regions.

Soviet Europe includes only one-quarter of the area of the Union, but here live three-quarters of the people. Not all are Great Russians, not all are even Slavs, for there are many pockets of other nationalities. Within the two million square miles between the Baltic and the Urals are many landscapes; boreal in the north, subtropical in the south. Each provides a distinct habitat.

The term "Europe" is surrounded by so much uncertainty that it may be well to discuss its eastern limit. As Parker has written:

> Controversy and confusion over the eastern boundary of Europe are as old as the name itself. Such confusion was inevitable after the western extremities of the Eurasian land mass had come, mainly through geographical ignorance, to be considered as a separate continent. This confusion could only become worse confounded when the word Europe, besides its use as a geographical name, began to express a distinctive culture or community of fluctuating extent.*

Many eastern boundaries have been proposed, ranging from the Ob to the Vistula. In some terms, Europe begins at the western limits of Soviet territory, thus making it western peninsular Eurasia. Europe and the U.S.S.R. would thus form separate subcontinents or realms. Soviet geographers have long debated the question, and their decision is that Europe begins at the eastern base of the Urals and the north slopes of the Caucasus. Since it is Soviet policy to appear European to Europeans and Asian to Asiatics, this division enables the country to have a base in each continent. Perhaps it is necessary to think of two Europes, Western and Eastern; one the peninsular maritime area of traditional European culture, the other the more continental Russian half.

Soviet Europe contains these geographic regions: Ukrainia; Byelorussia; the Baltic States; Metropolitan Leningrad; the Kola-Karelia Taiga; the Dvina-Pechora Taiga; the Central Agricultural Region;

* W. H. Parker: "Europe: How Far?", *Geographical Journal*, CXXVI, p. 278 (1960).

Metropolitan Moscow; the Southern Agricultural Region; and the Urals.

Ukrainia

The history of this region has been long and stormy; Ukrainia has been invaded by Turks, Mongols, Poles, Lithuanians, and Germans, as well as by Great Russians. Eighty per cent of the people are Ukrainian or Little Russian in nationality, with cultural and ethnic modifications which trace back to the borderland location.

While the bulk of the geographic region here considered lies within the Ukrainian Republic, the region takes in for convenience the small Moldavian Republic to the southwest and also the eastern extension of the Donets coal field where it continues beyond the political boundary. This larger region is here termed Ukrainia; it covers 200,000 square miles.

In size, population, and productivity, the Ukraine is somewhat comparable with France, but whereas the latter has maritime relations, the Ukraine tends to be continental in its climate and outlook.

The Ukrainian Soviet Socialist Republic is more important than it might appear on a map. Although it covers but one-fiftieth of the area of the Union, it accounts for one-fifth of the population, one-fifth of the farmland, one-quarter of the wheat, one-third of the coal, and one-half of the steel. Small wonder that it generates one-third of the railway traffic.

Although the economic center of gravity of the Union has shifted from the Ukraine toward the Urals, the Ukraine retains a unique significance in Soviet agriculture and industry. No other part of the Union has such rich soil, such developed natural resources, or such a dense population.

LANDFORMS AND GEOGRAPHIC REGIONS (*map on following pages*)

Geographic regions should represent over-all unity, both physical and cultural. They are mapped on a landform base to suggest that economic activities have their roots in environmental conditions. The initials represent the regional names used in this and the following chapters.

Soviet Europe includes Ukrainia, Byelorussia, Baltic States, Metropolitan Leningrad, Kola-Karelia Taiga, Dvina-Pechora Taiga, Central Agricultural Region, Metropolitan Moscow, Southern Agricultural Region, and the Urals.

Middle Asia is made up of Caucasia, Caspian Desert, Pamirs, Turan Oases, and Aral-Balkhash Deserts.

Siberia includes West Siberian Agricultural Region, Altai-Sayan Mountains, Ob Taiga, Yenisei Taiga, Arctic Fringe, Baikalia, Lena Taiga, Northeastern Mountains, Far East, and Sakhalin with the Kuriles.

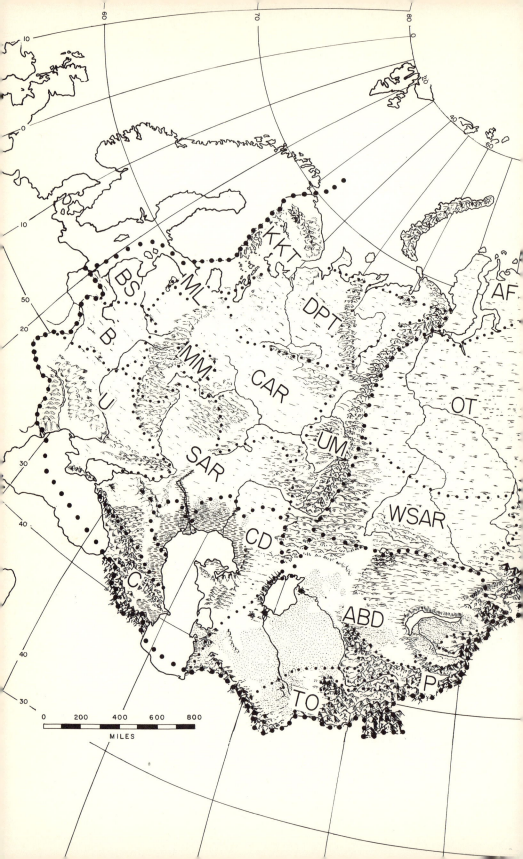

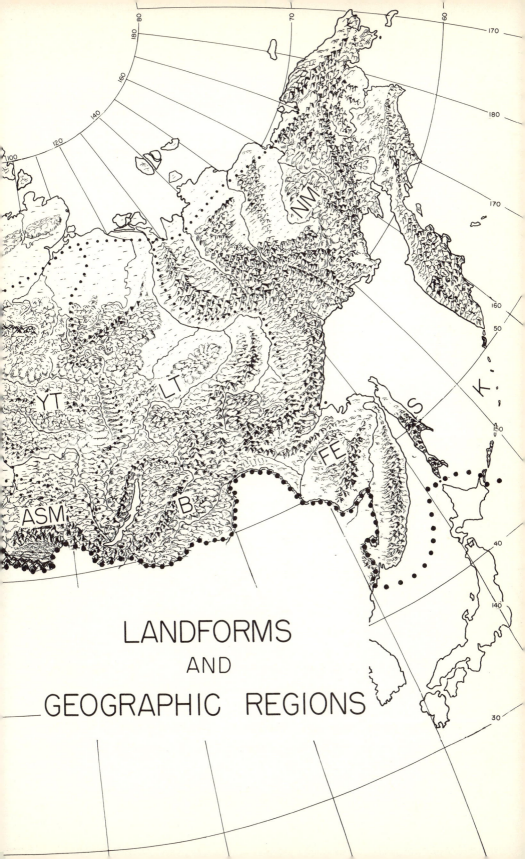

LANDFORMS
AND
GEOGRAPHIC REGIONS

Ukrainia occupies the south of Soviet Europe, but it is important to realize that much of it lies north of latitudes in the United States. If superimposed on North America the region would bisect the United States-Canadian boundary. Kiev and Kharkov both lie north of the 49th parallel. In a broad sense, Ukrainian conditions of climate, vegetation, soils, and crops resemble the Great Plains of Montana and Saskatchewan.

Most of the region is low in elevation, a land of broad plains and rolling hills. The edges of the Carpathians appear in the west, and long escarpments extend to the southeast; elsewhere the surface is nearly featureless. Through the center flows the Dnieper River, third largest in Europe and navigable to above Kiev. To the west are the Bug and Dniester, while in the east are the Don and its tributary, the Donets. A veneer of gently dipping sedimentary formations covers most of the region, except where windows expose underlying crystalline rocks.

The courses of the rivers reflect the geologic structures. Where harder beds outcrop, these form one-sided hills or low escarpments, several hundred feet high on the northeastern sides but with gentle dip slopes to the southwest. At Kiev, the Dnieper hugs the base of the escarpment along its southwestern or right-hand bank, and has a flood plan 10 miles wide on its left. This tendency for steep right-hand banks is a characteristic of all rivers at high latitudes, North America included. After following this escarpment to the southeast for 250 miles, the Dnieper abruptly cuts through the hills and makes a 90-degree turn to the southwest.

Summers are hot, for insolation and dry winds from interior Asia bring uncomfortable temperatures, as high as 95° F. Winters are cold, since Arctic air masses sweep across the plains without obstruction and the thermometer frequently records –20° F. Rivers are frozen for several months.

Agriculture prospers during the long hot summer days, provided that there is sufficient moisture. Here is one of Ukrainia's problems, for the average precipitation decreases from 24 inches in the northwest to 14 inches near the Black Sea. The first figure would be barely adequate in the United States, but with lower evaporation in the Soviet Union it is sufficient; unfortunately, rainfall varies from year to year, so that periods of crop failure have been recurrent. With but 14 inches of precipitation, agriculture is almost impossible without irrigation.

The Ukraine is famous for its rich black chernozem soils. These are among the most fertile on earth, but are a byproduct of the marginal rainfall and thus are not dependable for agriculture. Chernozem soils owe their fertility to the accumulation of subsurface humus from decaying grass roots, and to the limited extent of chemical leaching which results from the low rainfall. If the rainfall were higher the soils would be less fertile, though perhaps safer for cultivation. Similar soils in North America extend from Canada to Texas; where carelessly plowed in drier years, dust bowl conditions have developed. The Ukraine faces the same problem of wind erosion.

In the center of the region, where chernozem soils dominate, winter wheat is the great crop, supplemented by corn, sugar beets, soy beans, sunflower seeds, hemp or flax, and barley. Farther north, where the soils are podsolic, the chief crops are rye, oats, and potatoes. The drier south, with chestnut-brown soils, raises irrigated cotton and rice, along with some grains produced with dry-farming techniques.

If this agricultural aspect may be termed the Green Ukraine, there is also a Black Ukraine based on coal and industry. Here are high grade coals, natural gas, excellent iron ore, first class manganese, mercury, salt, kaolin, and clay for fire bricks. In addition there is hydroelectric power. Even more fortunate is the close occurrence of these industrial potentials, for the most part not more than 200 miles apart. Few areas on earth are better equipped for heavy industry; in Western Europe only the lower Rhine or the British Midlands are as fortunate.

The Donets coal field outcrops along the river of the same name. It has an extent from west to east of 230 miles, and measures 50 miles in width. Here are several hundred mines and a dozen important cities, only a few of which lie east of the political limits of the Ukrainian Republic. Many types of coal are present, including varieties which make good metallurgical coke.

Large amounts of iron ore are produced at Kirvoi Rog, 200 miles west of the coal, comparable in quality to that obtained near Lake Superior. Blast furnaces operate near both coal and iron. but chiefly at such coal centers as Donets and Makeevka. Krivoi Rog opened

---

MAJOR ECONOMIC REGIONS (*map on following pages*)

Planning underlies all Soviet economy, and the region is the working unit. The above Major Economic Regions form the basis for long term development. There are ten within the Russian Republic, three in the Ukraine, one for Kazakhstan, and three inter-republic regions, a total of seventeen major regions, each divided into a number of regions to a total of over 100. In addition, Byelorussia and Moldavia are separate administrative areas. (*Soviet Geography*, II #8, Oct. 1961, 84–88.)

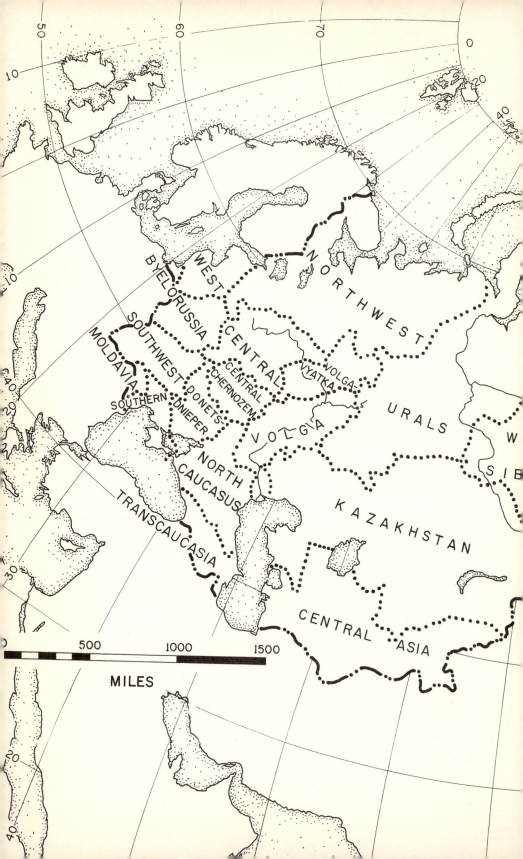

WEST

BYELORUSSIA

NORTHWEST

MOLDAVIA

SOUTHWEST

CENTRAL

VYATKA

VOLGA-

URALS

CENTRAL
CHERNOZEM

CENTRAL

DONETS-

SOUTHERN DNIEPER

VOLGA

W

SIB

NORTH
CAUCASUS

KAZAKHSTAN

TRANSCAUCASIA

CENTRAL ASIA

500   1000   1500

MILES

50   60   70   0

10

20

40

10

40

20

30

20

40

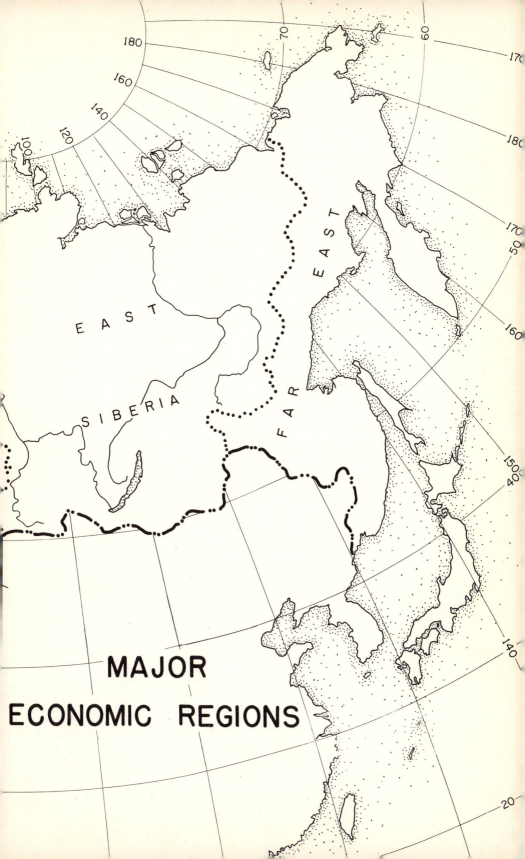

MAJOR
ECONOMIC REGIONS

the world's largest blast furnace in 1960. Halfway between the coal and iron ore is the hydroelectricity of the Dnieper dams; this is thus a convenient point for the production of electric furnace alloy steels.

In addition to the east-west movement of iron ore and coal between Donets and Krivoi Rog, there is a northward circulation from the Donets coal field based on the iron of the Kursk Magnetic Anomaly, and a southward movement to the low-grade ore on the Crimean peninsula at Kerch.

These raw materials help to make the Ukraine a major focus of heavy industry, probably among the half dozen most important producers on

UKRAINIA

	DONETS COAL BASIN
■	COAL MINES
Fe	IRON ORE
Mn	MANGANESE
▲	OIL
△	GAS
✦	HYDROELECTRICITY

0   25   50   75   100
MILES

UKRAINIA

Donets coal, and iron ore from Krivoi Rog, Kerch, and Kursk, plus manganese from Nikopol and electricity from the Dnieper, have helped to make the southern Ukraine one of the great industrial centers of the world. Kiev, Kharkov, and Volgagrad are the leading centers outside the coal basin. The number of railway tracks is indicated by the cross ties.

earth. The Donets Basin, especially, is a center of Soviet power. Giant furnaces furnish steel for great locomotive works. Cement and chemical plants supply half of Soviet Europe. This is a prime area for steel rails, railway equipment, trucks, farm machinery, and many types of basic production.

No region of the Union is so urbanized as Ukrainia; here as elsewhere cities are growing rapidly. In the 1959 census, two dozen urban centers had populations in excess of 100,000. (Census data may be found in the Appendix.)

Kiev ranks next to Moscow and Leningrad in size, with a population of well over a million. The city is known as "the mother of all the towns of Russia," for it dates from the ninth century. Christianity gained an early foothold, and in czarist days the city was a great center for pilgrimages, especially to the sacred convent of Lavra with

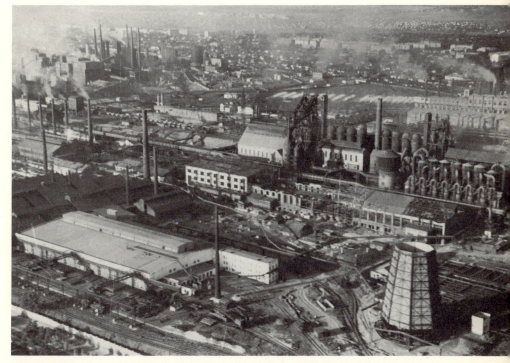

The proximity of coking coal, iron ore, and markets enabled the Ukraine to become the Union's leading center of heavy industry. This is a view of the Makeevka steel plant in the Donets coal basin. (*Courtesy Soviet Embassy, Washington*)

its catacombs. The city has been sacked and destroyed eight or ten times, and both World Wars brought devastation.

The city has a splendid location on hills which overlook the navigable Dnieper River. Greek and Norse traders met here a thousand years ago when Kiev was on the trade route from the Baltic to the Black Sea. Kiev's position on a river in the midst of a rich agricultural area might be compared to that of Regina in Canada.

The Ukraine is the Union's breadbasket and Kiev, the capital, lies near the center of the Republic. Industrial Kiev thus reflects the agricultural countryside. While the Republic has iron ore and coal, these lie elsewhere and have but slightly influenced Kiev. Instead, this is a city of light industries such as flour and sugar mills, tanneries and shoe factories, and textile plants. Machine industries are represented in ship-

The ancient city of Kiev lies on the high right-hand bank of the navigable Dnieper River, overlooking the broad flood plain. (*Courtesy Intourist*)

building and railroad yards. The road, water, and rail facilities which
focus on Kiev make it a natural center for collecting and distributing
products for its market area.

Kiev has grown more slowly than some cities and makes less of a
contribution to the national economy, but it remains a city of great
traditional importance in politics and education. Its architectural heri-
tage is reflected in a familiar saying which credits Moscow with
strength, Leningrad with skill, and Kiev with beauty.

Kharkov is about the same size as Kiev, but is quite different, since
it is a city of machine industry. The city does not lie near iron or
coal fields, nor does it have blast furnaces; these are a hundred miles
or more away. Industrial Kharkov is something of a parasite to the
Donets Basin. The city lies 450 miles south from Moscow, roughly
halfway to the Black Sea. Its river is unnavigable, but there are half
a dozen rail lines.

Unlike Kiev with its thousand years of history, Kharkov dates from
1654. In place of old monasteries and historic sights, the visitor finds

The harbor of Odessa carries little international commerce but is an important
fishing center for the Black Sea. Grain elevators and flour mills reflect the agricultural life of the Ukraine. (*Courtesy Soviet Embassy, Washington*)

giant factories and new commercial buildings. Like Kiev, Kharkov
suffered terrible German invasions during both World Wars. On several occasions it has replaced Kiev as the capital of the Ukraine.

The production of machinery in Kharkov includes an impressive
array of tractors and trucks, farm implements, locomotives and railway equipment, machine tools, bicycles, and electrical apparatus both
large and small. Various chemicals are made from coal. Because of the
agricultural countryside, there are also factories for food and clothing.
The Five Year Plans, with their stress on industrialization, brought
boom prosperity to Kharkov. The population has quadrupled since the
revolution.

The major city of southwest Ukrainia is Odessa, picturesque seaport
on the Black Sea. In the days when Russia had a free international
economy, Odessa was the nation's second seaport. So it may still be,
but the over-all volume of foreign trade is so low that neither Leningrad
nor Odessa ranks among the world's 50 leading ports. Whereas Leningrad handled imports of machinery and specialized products, Odessa
shipped wheat and agricultural items.

Even though the city lies on the Black Sea far in the south of Soviet
Europe, its harbor is frozen for six weeks each winter. This is not surprising when one finds that the Black Sea is on a parallel with Lake
Superior, and that Odessa matches Duluth. The harbor is large and
deep; in the years before the revolution it handled seven hundred ships
a year. Today, few foreign passenger steamers call at Odessa, and non-
Soviet freighters are chiefly tramp ships. The city does have a considerable volume of Soviet shipping to other Black Sea ports, and to
Vladivostok. Industries include food products, agricultural machinery,
and the evaporation of sea water for salt.

The second seaport of the region, actually east of the political limits
of the Ukraine but within the same geographic area, is Rostov-on-Don.
Flour mills and tanneries process agricultural products from the Don
Basin, and a large fishing industry is based on the near-by Sea of Azov.
Since Rostov is about the same distance from the Donets industrial area
as Kharkov, Rostov also draws on it for raw material, in this case for
the manufacture of agricultural equipment.

Within the Donets Basin are a number of important cities. Each of
them is a coal mining center, and most have giant blast furnaces oper-
ating on iron ore from Krivoi Rog, Kursk, or Kerch. Three such
centers are Donets (formerly Stalino), Makeevka, and Lugansk, each a
Soviet Pittsburgh.

Grouped around the Dnieper rapids are a series of industrial centers.

The city of Zaporozhe lies near the country's first large dam, while to the north are Dnepropetrovsk and Dneprodzerzhinsk. Electrochemical plants, aluminum refining, and steel mills are the chief industries.

Byelorussia

The Byelorussian Soviet Socialist Republic, sometimes known as White Russia, lies in one of the poorest and most backward parts of Soviet Europe. Rural settlements cluster on sand dunes, natural levees along the rivers, or higher places in the glacial drift. Population distribution is uneven; some areas average less than two people per square mile, while in others the average rises to 150. The White Russians, perhaps so called because of their traditional white clothing, represent one of the purest of the Slavic groups; many have lived here since the thirteenth century, when they fled into the swamplands to escape the Tatar invasion.

The geographic region here considered, about the same as the political area, covers 125,000 square miles, more than half that of Ukrainia, but the population and productivity are much lower. Byelorussia

Flax is an important crop in Byelorussia and the northwestern R.S.F.S.R. where much of the soil tends to be acid. (*Sovfoto*)

occupies the hilly headwaters of the south-draining Dnieper and Pripet and the north-flowing Western Dvina and other streams tributary to the Baltic. One-tenth of the region is bog or lake land. In some areas lakes and channels are so extensive that most travel is by boat. Road construction presents problems, since rock and gravel are scarce, but a modern canal links the Pripet and Bug rivers and provides for barge service westward into Germany.

Fishing is important, and peat is extracted from many bogs. Large areas of wet lands have been reclaimed for agriculture, but soils tend to be acid. The chief grains are rye and oats, while root crops such as beets, turnips and potatoes are widely grown. Hemp and flax are traditional fibers.

Because the Baltic Sea is near by, the rainfall is generally adequate and drought is rare. This is an area of mixed forests, with hardwoods such as oak and maple mixed with conifers such as spruce and fir. Hemlock and oak supply tanbark for the leather industry.

Lack of mineral resources hampers industrial activity, and most of the rivers are too sluggish for generating power, so that peat is the chief source of energy.

Minsk, with a population of over half a million, is the capital and hence a political and cultural center. Its industries include leather factories, paper mills, woodworking plants, and food-processing factories.

Baltic States

The three Union republics which border the Baltic have a traditional two-way orientation. Estonia, Latvia, and Lithuania face westward toward the cultures of Scandinavia and Germany, and eastward economically to interior Russia. In addition to the three Soviet Socialist Republics, the geographic region includes the area around Kaliningrad, once Prussian Koenigsburg but now a part of the R.S.F.S.R. No other part of the U.S.S.R. has had such extensive contacts with the modern world; as a result the Baltic States have a higher level of material prosperity than prevails to the east. Thus the state of education and urban developments is transitional between the interior and the lands west and south of the Baltic Sea. In some ways Latvia appears to be more advanced than either Estonia or Lithuania.

These Baltic peoples are Protestants and Roman Catholics, in contrast to the Great Russians who are or were Russian Orthodox. In one sense, the eastern border of the Republics might form a valid boundary between Western Europe and the Soviet realm.

Each of the three republics is a national unit, distinct in history, language, culture, and ethnography. These might furnish grounds for political independence if it were not for their strategic position between the great continental area of the Soviet Union and that country's need for contact with the Atlantic. Provided that full consideration is given to minority cultures, large continental countries are entitled to free access to the ocean.

The Baltic States, like all of the Russian borderlands, have had a stormy history. Control has alternated between Danish, Swedish, Polish, German, and Russian conquests. At one period the Baltic Sea became a Swedish lake.

Each of the three nations has had its periods of expansion and grandeur, as when Lithuania extended to the Black Sea in the fourteenth century. Estonia and Latvia were added to the Russian Empire in 1721, and Lithuania was annexed in 1795. Until the First World War they continued as integral parts of czarist territory, and their seaports were linked to Russian economy by a network of railways. Despite Russian attempts to impose her culture, each area retained much of its traditional language and customs.

Following the revolution which set up the Soviet Union, Estonia, Latvia, and Lithuania declared their independence. This freedom continued until the close of the Second World War, when they were unilaterally reannexed by the U.S.S.R., each as a separate republic.

The typical landscape is that left by the continental ice sheets. Adjoining the Gulf of Finland is a belt of eskers; to the south of them lie exceptionally well-developed drumlins, some of the finest in the world. Undulating glacial ground moraine covers most of the remaining area, with innumerable lakes. Drainage is considerably better than in the marshlands of Byelorussia to the south. Most of the area lies below 500 feet.

Peat deposits occur in some of the lower areas, and peat is used widely as fuel. Estonia has oil shales, but except for some limestone and phosphate, there are few other mineral resources.

No other part of Soviet Europe is so much exposed to marine influences or has such a low range between summer and winter temperatures. Polar air masses nevertheless invade the area during the winter months to bring cold periods. The growing season varies from 120 to 180 days. Between 20 and 25 inches of rain falls annually, of which a considerable part occurs as snow. Sections near the sea are damp and cloudy, particularly in winter.

This is a long-settled land, and most of the good soil is utilized for crops of rye, oats, barley, wheat, and flax. Soils tend to be acid and podsolic so that crop yields are low. Dairying is widespread in each of the three republics, and stock breeding and poultry keeping are more profitable than grain growing in some sections. Since climatic conditions improve southward, agriculture is least developed in Estonia. The principal exports are timber and wood products, flax and linseed oil, and dairy products.

Most industries rest directly on agriculture and forestry. Twenty per cent of the region is covered by forests, and an efficient system of forest control and development insures permanence of this resource.

The acquisition of the Baltic States not only gives the Soviet Union a better frontier in the west but also makes available the port of Riga, near the mouth of the Western Dvina River. This city, which in 1951 celebrated the 750th anniversary of its founding, has important textile and metal industries.

Metropolitan Leningrad

The city of Peter the Great, now named after Lenin, lies on the swampy delta of the Neva River, facing the Baltic. Here was Peter's "Window to Europe," a planned city of magnificent boulevards and splendid government buildings. Some of these have deteriorated under the Soviets, but the art collections of the Hermitage and the Winter Palace are still among the greatest in the world. Under the present government the collections have been enlarged by the addition of paintings and statuary once scattered among the homes of the nobility. All of the great masters are represented, with more Rembrandts than anywhere else on earth.

Prior to 1703, the area of Leningrad belonged to Sweden. In that year Peter the Great defeated the Swedes and gave his country its first seaport, as well as providing Europe with a front door to Russia. Still earlier, near-by Novgorod was a member of the Hanseatic League.

Few cities have a poorer actual site, or a better general location than Leningrad. The delta of the Neva River is so swampy that thousands of workmen lost their lives in constructing Peter's new capital. All large buildings rest on piles, for the ground is too soft for normal foundations. There are so many canals and distributaries in the Neva delta that the city needs 500 bridges.

Leningrad lies close to sea level, and part of it may be inundated when the river is in flood, or when west winds pile up water in the shallow Gulf of Finland. The river is frozen from mid-November till early April. Although the city is 400 miles north of Moscow, winter temperatures are 5° F. warmer because of the nearness to the sea. Leningrad lies two-thirds of the way from the equator to the pole, so that during the long summer evenings there is enough light to read a

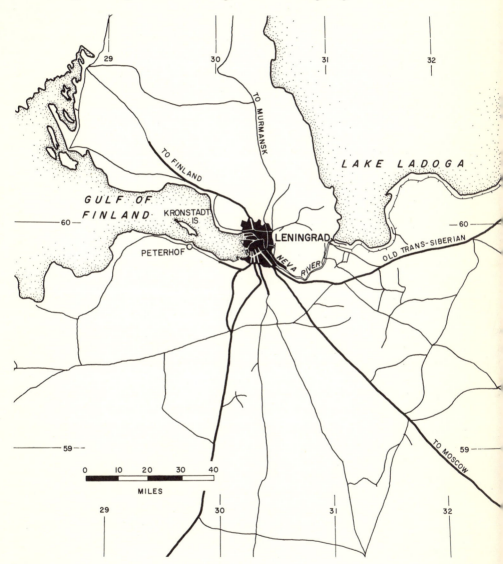

LENINGRAD

Leningrad lies on the swampy delta of the Neva River where it empties into the Baltic. To the east is Lake Ladoga, and through it canal boats may reach the headwaters of the Volga. Railways are shown in heavy lines for multiple tracks, and in thin lines for single-track facilities.

newspaper at midnight. Twilight merges into dawn, for the sun barely sinks below the northern horizon; people walk the streets till well after midnight. Winter days are correspondingly short and cold, and it is dark until 10 a.m. and after 3 p.m. Two hundred days a year have rain or snow.

If the city is handicapped by its immediate site, it profits from its regional setting. Sea lanes lead to Scandinavia, Germany, and the Atlantic. The Neva provides water links via the Mariinsk Canal system to the headwaters of the Volga, and also to the Dnieper; and via the Baltic-White Sea Canal to the Arctic. These, and the land routes which have long focused on the city, made czarist St. Petersburg the natural outlet for the northern half of European Russia, the Urals, Central Asia, and even Siberia.

Since St. Petersburg was both the chief seaport and the seat of government, here was where foreign concerns established warehouses and sought business concessions. Domestic industry was dependent on imported machinery and supplies which were available only here. As commerce grew, St. Petersburg developed assembly plants and factories. As a result, this was the first city to have skilled mechanics for making typewriters, electrical apparatus, textile machinery, chemicals, and machine tools. This skill has become traditional, and today no city in the Union can duplicate Leningrad's reservoir of highly specialized workers. Leningrad trade-marks rank high all across the country.

It was not an accident that the Revolution of 1917 took place in Leningrad. This was not merely because it was the capital; Marxism emphasizes the revolutionary role of the factory proletariat, and Leningrad had the largest bloc of such workers.

Leningrad is a very different city from Moscow. The latter grew without plan, the former was planned *de novo*. Peter laid out a regal city, with broad thoroughfares and splendid vistas. The main streets are lined with elaborate buildings, planned in groups or ensembles. Along the main street, the Nevski Prospekt, the buildings average five stories in height, many of them designed by Italian architects.

Although Moscow has long played a dominant role in Russian history, St. Petersburg was for two centuries the center of national culture. The new capital drew to itself the aristocracy of arts and literature, and here developed the great traditions in music and the theatre. The czar was a patron of the Russian Orthodox Church—perhaps too much so, since official religion became a tool of the state. Leningrad has many magnificent churches, such as the Cathedral of St. Isaacs, erected a century ago at the then astonishing cost of 23,000,000 rubles. Its gilded dome rises 333 feet.

Baltic ports are closed by ice for several months each winter. This is a view of the first atomic-powered ship, the icebreaker *Lenin* in the harbor of Leningrad. (*Courtesy U.S.S.R. National Committee, I.G.U.*)

When Peter the Great had his headquarters here, he built a beautiful summer palace to the west of the city in the fashion of Versailles. This was known as Peterhof. Destroyed during the last war, it has been rebuilt. Cascades, fountains, and gilded statues decorate a fabulous park. Much of Leningrad's glamour has gone with the disappearance of court life, and through the early tendency of the Soviets to "punish" the city for having been the seat of the czar, but some of the grandeur remains.

The city now accounts for one-eighth of the country's industrial output, as compared with Moscow's one-sixth. This includes a variety of electrical machinery such as large turbines and generators, telephone

Three Soviet cities have subway systems: Moscow, Leningrad, and Kiev. This is a view of one of the ornate stations on the Leningrad "Metro." (*Courtesy U.S.S.R. National Committee, I.G.U.*)

and radio equipment, precision machines, chemicals, rubber goods, paper, furniture, cotton textiles, and the nation's largest shipyards. The nearest coal lies in the Pechora Valley, 1,000 miles to the northeast, but near-by peat contributes fuel for thermoelectric plants.

Soviet foreign commerce is sharply limited and Leningrad is no longer a major world seaport. This is in sharp contrast to conditions when Russia was open to free commerce. In those days coal came from Wales, machinery from Germany, jute from India, raw cotton from the United States, and rubber from the tropics, in addition to manufactured products from the Western World.

Kola-Karelia Taiga

Each of the regions so far discussed has been affected by continental glaciation. Very little of the Ukraine was invaded, but outwash deposits and wind-blown silt are important. The confused topography of Byelorussia represents the terminal dumps of the ice sheets. The Baltic States were areas of both glacial erosion and deposition. Karelia and the Kola Peninsula represent the core area of ice radiation, with intense scour. Innumerable glacial lakes, usually connected by swift rivers, cover 10 per cent of the region. Most of the area is hilly and lies within 1,000 feet of sea level; isolated mountains rise to 3,400 feet.

In a rough sense, this glacial sequence across the Soviet Union corresponds to a cross-section southward from the Canadian Shield. Karelia is underlain by the same kind of ancient crystalline and metamorphic rocks which are present around Hudson's Bay, and the rounded topography which results from ice action is similar. Drainage has been deranged, the ancient soil cover is gone, and there are many smooth rock outcrops. The Gulf of Finland, and lakes Ladoga and Onega, represent glacially scoured basins akin to the American Great Lakes. The Baltic States, with their drumlins, match Northern New York, while the lake country of Byelorussia finds similarities in upper Michigan and Minnesota. The Ukraine is a cooler replica of Kansas with its loess.

The Karelian taiga is an eastward continuation of the Finnish forests, and for some years its ethnic character led it to be organized as the Karelian Soviet Socialist Republic, one of the 16 union republics then in existence. The Kola Peninsula, to the north, has a transition from taiga to tundra. The two areas have a combined area of 100,000 square miles.

Southern Karelia once had a splendid forest of pine, spruce, and birch. This has been extensively cut over, in part for export through Leningrad. Farther north large forest areas remain, with decreasing quality, related to the shorter frost-free period and decreased precipitation. The growing season is approximately 100 days. Rainfall diminishes from 24 inches in the south to 16 inches in the north, much of it coming in the late summer. Snow falls from October through May.

Agricultural conditions are unfavorable except in the extreme south, where hay and fodder crops support a dairy industry. Specialized farms supply fresh vegetables for the people of several new urban centers. Cabbages and turnips mature during the long summer hours of sunshine, but acres of greenhouses are necessary for other crops.

Large-scale mining operations have developed in the Kola Peninsula, especially in the low Khibin Mountains. This area contains a number of unique minerals, notably apatite which is a phosphate mineral used as a base for fertilizer, and nepheline, a source of aluminum analogous to bauxite. In both cases reserves appear to be the largest in the world. Nickel and copper deposits are also extensive.

Murmansk is the Union's only year-around seaport. It lies 20 miles from the sea on a deep fiord where the warmth of the Atlantic Drift keeps the Arctic open throughout the year. The harbor provided a valuable gateway to Russia in wartime, but otherwise handles only negligible international commerce. Fishing is important, especially for cod and haddock. Murmansk serves as the western terminus of the Northern Sea Route, and is also a naval base. By means of canals and the Volga, small naval vessels may be moved from the Arctic to the Black Sea. The city has a population of a quarter of a million, making it the largest city in the world at this high latitude. The Polar Arrow Express train covers the 900 miles from Leningrad to Murmansk in 38 hours.

Dvina-Pechora Taiga

The eastern half of Soviet Europe may be conveniently divided into three geographical regions. In the north is the Dvina-Pechora Taiga, largely an uncleared area with Arctic drainage. In the center and occupying the upper Volga basin is the Central Agricultural Region, once forested but now mostly cleared. To the south is the Southern Agricultural Region covering the dry grasslands of the lower Volga and Don valleys.

The Northern Dvina and the Pechora are the chief north-flowing rivers between the Kola Peninsula and the Urals. Whereas Karelian forests were once the main sources of lumber, the Dvina-Pechora Taiga is now the chief export area.

The region occupies about 500,000 square miles between Lake Ladoga and the Urals, and north of the Arctic-Volga watershed which lies near latitude 60° N. Here is the country's finest coniferous forest, made up of Norway spruce, Scotch pine, larch, and fir, with scattered birch, alder, and willow. Trees grow slowly, so that 18-inch logs may be 150 years old. Most lumber within easy access of each navigable river has already been cut, but vast forests remain in the interior. This is especially true along the Pechora where lumbering operations are more recent. Products of the Dvina-Pechora Taiga include sawed lumber, railroad ties, mine props, and pulpwood.

The population is scanty, and largely confined to the river basins. Villages lie on the borders of rivers or lakes, or occupy the slopes of marainic hills away from the damp lowlands. Hay, dairy products, and vegetables provide the chief agricultural income. In the south it is possible to raise fair crops of barley, rye, oats, flax, and hemp.

The leading city of the region is Arkhangelsk, the shipping center, located on the delta of the Northern Dvina where it enters the White

Sea. The city lies near the Arctic Circle, in the latitude of Nome, Alaska, but has a population of over 250,000. The White Sea is frozen from November through April but icebreakers keep the port open during most of the winter. The river is frozen for 180 days a year, and is subject to severe floods when the ice goes out each spring. Arkhangelsk lies on a distributary of the Northern Dvina some 25 miles from the sea, and has a channel which is dredged to 21 feet. The annual average temperature is only 33° F., and for six months the thermometer is below freezing.

Central Agricultural Area

The divide between Arctic and Volga drainage is low and does not mark any major change in climate or natural vegetation. The difference lies in accessibility, the extent of cleared forest, and the development of agriculture. Whereas the Dvina-Pechora Taiga is agriculturally a hay and dairy area, the Central Agricultural Region is a land of grain crops.

The region reaches from the western limits of the R.S.F.S.R. to the Urals, and southward from around latitude 60° N., somewhat north of the Trans-Siberian Railway, to the border between forest and steppe. The latter is an irregular line, between latitudes 52° and 54° N., which bends southward in the Kursk and Volga hills and swings north along the Don and Volga lowlands.

Almost the entire region is drained by the Volga and its main tributaries, the Oka and the Kama. This is the greatest river system in Western Eurasia, and carries two-thirds of the river-borne freight of the Union. Extensive hydroelectric developments are under way, on both the Volga and the Kama, with a series of large dams and long narrow reservoirs.

Much of the region is an erosional plain, with slopes so gentle that floods do considerable damage. Elevations lie below 1,000 feet except in the Valdai, Smolensk-Moscow, and Pre-Volga hills. Most of the area was glaciated, but strong morainic features are limited to the northwest quarter.

Farming is the dominant activity, for this is the heart of the agricultural triangle; more properly, the region occupies the northern half of the wide end of the triangle, balanced by the steppe lands farther south. The rainfall amounts to 20 inches, which is enough for normal cultivation. Crop yields are often related to the amount and gradual melting of the winter snows, and to the proper seasonal distribution of moisture. The frost-free period is from 120 to 150 days, and annual average temperatures range from 35° to 40° F. Although these conditions appear severe, they are considerably milder than in Canada at similar latitudes, where Hudson's Bay has but 60 days without frost.

Rye was once the chief crop, for it is tolerant of cool summers, short growing seasons, and podsol soils, but new varieties of spring wheat have pushed wheat cultivation northward so that in acreage wheat exceeds rye. Flax, sunflowers, potatoes, and cabbages are widely grown. Livestock includes cattle, sheep, goats, pigs and horses.

All of the area was once forested and large tracts of timber still remain, especially in the north and east. Even near Moscow half the area is forested. As woodlands are gradually cleared, cultivated fields increase. In natural terms, this is an area of mixed forest, with both conifers and hardwoods.

Most of the people are Russians, but in the east there are islands of Tatars, Bashkirs, Chuvash and other Mongoloid groups, several of whom have their own autonomous political areas. Rural population densities vary from 25 to 250 people per square mile, in part a reflection of variations in soil and drainage. In view of the rather inhospitable environment and low food-producing potentials, these densities represent moderate crowding.

Many of the major cities lie along the Volga, either at river junctions or at rail crossings. The westernmost is the city of Kalinin, on the railway from Moscow to Leningrad. Downstream is the historic city of Yaroslavl, the oldest Russian settlement on the Volga and at the crossing of the Trans-Siberian Railway. Gorki, at the junction of the Oka, a city of about a million people, was formerly known as Nizhni Novgorod. The city was once famous for its annual fair where merchants from the East brought goods for buyers from the West. Kazan lies near the junction with the Kama; below it is Ulyanovsk.

Each city of the region processes the forest or agricultural products of its hinterland; thus Kazan is famous for its leather goods, Kalinin weaves linen textiles, while Gorki makes furniture and paper, and is also a center for agricultural machinery. Flour mills operate in many towns, while sugar from beets, leather, and clothing are also important. Every river has its lumber mills.

Metropolitan Moscow

Few cities in the world have the rich history or cultural fascination of Moscow. The city dates back at least to the year 1147. A decade later the first wooden palisade was built around the town. It is now a city of over 6,000,000 people in the metropolitan area. So important is the city that it is here treated as a separate geographic region.

Although English-speaking foreigners call the city Moscow, the proper romanization would be Moskva.

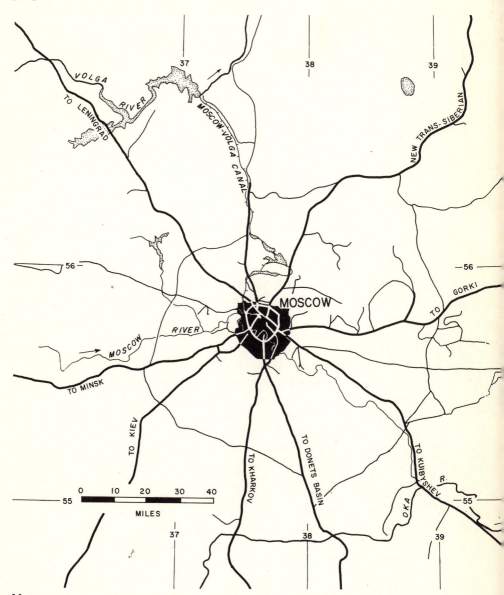

Moscow

Moscow is the focal point for eleven railways, linked by circular lines within the city and in an outer ring. By means of the Moscow–Volga Canal, boat services extend northward to Leningrad and southward to Astrakhan and Rostov-on-Don.

In the early years, Moscow was an important stopping point on the trade routes from the Baltic to the Caspian. In the fifteenth century, the unification of Russia centered on Moscow, as successive czars gave unity to the state. Their chief enemies were the Lithuanians on the west and the Golden Horde of Mongols from the east. In 1812 the city was captured by Napoleon, but climate and space, plus Russian resistance, were too much for him. Although often attacked, or destroyed by great fires, each time the city has been rebuilt.

Today Moscow dominates the Union of Soviet Socialist Republics. Few other capitals in the world combine so much history, so much glamour, so much political power, or so much industrial importance for so many people. This is indeed a fascinating and significant city. On its streets one may see Cossacks from the Volga, Uzbeks from Middle Asia, and Yakuts from the Siberian Arctic, all in their colorful national dress.

There is no city in North America which matches Moscow in location or importance. In latitude it lies 500 miles north of the United States-Canadian border, well north of Edmonton and beyond the limit of settlement in the Canadian Prairie Provinces. Continental extremes characterize summer and winter, with a range from 100° F. down to −40° F. The year-around temperature average is but 7° F. above freezing.

It was not inevitable that Moscow should have been built exactly where it is, but the immediate site does offer advantages. The city centers on a high bluff along the north bank of the meandering Moscow River. The countryside is broadly rolling, a part of the Central Agricultural Region.

Just as all roads led to Rome, so many Soviet roads and railways center on the capital. To see their evolution one needs to review the history of Moscow. At the point where the city developed, the Moscow River was easily crossed. Here was where early roads focused. And as with many such river crossings, here was where travelers stopped overnight or came for trade. This was the beginning of the Kremlin, a fortress town for merchants and local chiefs.

The Kremlin is the heart of historic Russia. The present structure was built shortly before the year 1500. The walls of red brick are capped by battlements like a medieval fortress. Above the five gates rise pointed towers, on top of which shine great ruby-colored stars. Each gate marked the road to a city, and the gates were so named, although the original destinations now carry different names. The importance of the Kremlin is suggested by an old saying: "There is nothing above Russia save Moscow, and nothing above Moscow save the Kremlin."

Since merchandise which passed through the gates was taxed, some traders found it better to display their wares outside the wall even though there might be danger from bandits. A large market developed to the east of the Kremlin, and from the color of the brick wall became known as the Red Square. This name long predates Soviet rule. As early Moscow grew, the walled enclosure became too small, and the Kremlin was increasingly taken over for political functions. Today it is a collection of palaces and cathedrals.

At one end of the Square is the bizarre Cathedral of St. Basil, built by Czar Ivan the Terrible 400 years ago. A dozen fantastic pineapple domes and onion spires are painted in all the colors of the rainbow. This monument to Russia's past is no longer a church, but it has been kept in excellent repair by the communists. Beside the Kremlin wall is the tomb where the body of Lenin lies in state.

To protect the Red Square and the homes which grew up around it, another wall was erected at a distance of half a mile. This is sometimes known as the Chinese Wall, although neither Chinese nor Mongols were involved. This wall also had gates, along the same radial roads as those which served the Kremlin.

Moscow increasingly became a meeting place between East and West, and the city continued to grow. The area outside the Chinese Wall came to be filled with shops and a maze of lanes. To enclose the expanding city, an earthen rampart was built, the so-called Garden Circle Wall. Still another circular wall was added by the first of the Romanoff Czars in the seventeenth century. The street plan of Moscow thus reveals its history as do the growth rings in the cross-section of a tree.

Present-day Moscow has burst these bounds and has spread for miles on both sides of the river. The old walls, except those of the Kremlin, have been torn down and replaced by circular boulevards. The radial roads still dominate the street pattern, with an assortment of ill-planned side streets between them.

Railways match the street patterns. Eleven lines focus on Moscow, with stations for several points of the compass. To link the lines, a circular railway parallels the outermost of the old walls. From the Kremlin as the focal point of the Union, it is an overnight trip northward to Leningrad and a day and a half farther to Murmansk. Or one may turn westward to Minsk and Riga, a day away; or southwest to Kiev and Odessa; or south to Kharkov and Baku; or eastward to

Sverdlovsk Square, facing the Bolshoi Opera House, is a center of urban activity in Moscow. (*Sovfoto*)

Kuibyshev, the Urals, and across Siberia to Irkutsk and Vladivostok, nine days distant.

While the Kremlin and the Red Square form the historic focus of Moscow, the active life of the city centers on another square near by, facing the Opera House. The theatrical arts, especially the ballet, have long received great emphasis in Russia, and the Soviet regime has continued the tradition of lavish government support. Near this square are the leading department stores and hotels.

Severe winters play havoc with the stucco which faces many Russian buildings. After a few years without repair they appear quite dilapidated. The Soviets have not yet learned how to make a stucco that sticks.

Pre-revolutionary Moscow was an overgrown village, with many rural characteristics. Residential and industrial areas were intermingled without plan. Transport and public utilities were seriously inadequate. Czarist Moscow had fewer than two million people; in thirty years the number has trebled.

Moscow is now in the process of major reconstruction. Large areas in the center of the city, and on the outskirts, have been replanned. New streets have been opened and many of the old winding lanes have ceased to exist. Eight skyscrapers dominate the skyline, up to 32 stories in height. It is not merely that new buildings replace the old; the street pattern has been remade. Few cities in modern times have been so redesigned. Along with these visible changes have come others in the field of water supply, sewers, central heating and electrical stations, and transportation.

Where old narrow streets were to be widened, business was allowed to continue in the front of the shops. The rear of the buildings on either side of the street were torn down and the new structures built, set back to face the widened boulevard. When these were ready, the old facades were removed and the new wide street was ready for use. Some of these streets have a distance from sidewalk to sidewalk of 200 feet.

With the rebuilding of the central area has gone the replanning of industry and the development of recreation. Along the river are parks, and green belts surround the outer city. All Moscow is not a city of beauty and light; slums remain, and narrow cobblestone lanes open off new boulevards. Nor is the new architecture all of the best. Old Moscow had renaissance and baroque buildings, reflecting the ornamental decoration of the Italians who influenced design under the czars; today, modernistic and neo-Babylonian forms are favored.

The Subway is the pride of the new Moscow. Several lines cross the center on diagonals and a circular line surrounds the central city. Other cities may provide better underground service, but none have more elaborate stations. Each has its own architectural treatment, with an extensive use of tile, stainless steel, or ornamental stone from the Urals. The initial line of the Subway was constructed during the 1930's when the Soviets were experimenting with the five-day week. There was no Saturday or Sunday holiday; each factory or office had one day in five as a free day. In order to dig the Subway, thousands of Moscovites gave their services during their free day. There was an element of compulsion in their volunteering, but there was also pride in accomplishment.

Transport by water has always played a large role in Russia. It is, of course, relatively cheap, and Soviet railways are so overloaded that

Modern Moscow has hundreds of apartment houses which look like these along Bolshaya Sadovaya Street. Privately owned passenger cars are uncommon. (*Courtesy Soviet Embassy, Washington*)

waterways are still important. The Moscow River was formerly too shallow for much navigation, and in summer the supply of water was insufficient for the needs of the city. The Moscow-Volga Canal now links the city with Volga commerce and insures adequate municipal water. The Moscow River flows into the Oka, and this in turn enters the Volga. Instead of canalizing this down-river section, a 75-mile canal connects the city with the upper Volga. So much additional water is now brought to Moscow that seven bridges had to be rebuilt.

Moscow is far from the ocean, but the Moscow-Volga Canal has brought visions of transport links something like those of Chicagoans toward the St. Lawrence and Illinois-Mississippi waterways. The upper Volga has long been connected with the Neva River which leads to Leningrad. This Mariinsk Canal system has several times been enlarged, and was further developed during the 1960's. Farther north, the Baltic-White Sea Canal connects Leningrad with the Arctic. In 1952 the lower Volga was linked with the Don River by a new canal near Stalingrad.

As a result of these canals, Moscow now advertises itself as "The Port of the Five Seas." To the north one may reach the Baltic and White seas. To the southeast is the Caspian, while through the Don boats may sail to the Azov and Black seas. Thus does the Union endeavor to burst its bounds of continentality.

Present-day Moscow is the political, cultural, commercial, and industrial center for the Union's people. Its only rival in size is Leningrad; its chief rival in industry is Kharkov. Nothing takes the place of the Kremlin as the center of ancient Russia and of the present-day Union; no city can match Moscow's seventy institutions of higher learning.

Moscow accounts for one-sixth of the country's manufacturing industry, and is the largest single industrial center. Near-by raw materials are limited to lignite, and the products of farm and forest. In the absence of minerals, heavy industry takes a secondary position, although there is a growing production of high-grade alloy steels. The major items in Moscow's production lie in the engineering field: automobiles, electrical goods, special steels, and machine tools. Other products come from chemical industries, textile manufacturing, printing, and light industries. The production of food and clothing supply work for many employees.

Southern Agricultural Region

In terms of soil, the agricultural possibilities of the lower Volga and Don are among the most attractive in the entire Union, but if judged by climate the story is very different. Before the arrival of man this was a steppe, treeless except along the streams or in the moister north. For centuries it was the home of nomadic horsemen, the Cossacks of the Volga, Don, and Kuban steppes. Into these grasslands came Mongol warriors, and later the Russian farmer.

The yearly precipitaton decreases from 20 inches in the west to as little as 12 inches in the southeast, with 16 inches a representative figure. Since low rainfall is associated with high variability, crop failures have been recurrent, sometimes reaching the proportions of a national calamity.

This is an area of rich black chernozem and the almost equally valuable chestnut-brown soils. Both are high in organic matter and soluble minerals, but their very fertility is caused by insufficient rainfall.

Successful agriculture depends on accumulating soil moisture through careful conservation of winter snow and frequent harrowing to check evaporation. Shelterbelt planting has been used with moderate success for decades. Irrigation developments include a great network of canals in the eastern Volga steppe and along the Don River.

Some of the largest state farms lie on the drier margins of agriculture in this region. Crop yields are too uncertain to be risked by collective farms, but by specialized techniques the government hopes to obtain a fair harvest in most years. In twenty average years at Saratov one may expect three years of complete crop failure and but five good harvests. Drought brings a risk to livestock as well as to grain.

Spring wheat and winter rye are the dominant grains, followed by oats, barley, and millet. The only other crop of importance is sunflower, raised for oil from its seeds.

Three large cities along the Volga dominate the economic life: Kuibyshev, Volgagrad, and Saratov. Each is the site of a huge dam and hydroelectric development. Three other river towns are of local importance as political and commercial centers: Voronezh on the upper Don, Penza on the Sura, and Chkalov (Orenburg) on the upper Ural River. Rostov-on-Don and Kursk might be included but have already been described as part of the larger Ukrainia.

Kuibyshev lies 500 miles southeast of Moscow, roughly the same distance from the capital as Leningrad, Minsk, Kiev, and Kharkov. Kuibyshev is about the mid-point along the Volga, and is one of the main railway crossings for east-west travel. The city lies near the northern limit of the black earth steppe in the midst of a rich agricultural zone.

Along much of its course, the Volga follows an open valley where dam construction is difficult. Above Kuibyshev an east-west elevation, the Zhiguli Hills, narrows the valley and it is here that the first huge Volga dam was constructed. When completed, its capacity of 2,100,000 kilowatts was the largest in the world. Some of the electric power is transmitted to Moscow, some is used in local industry and railways, and some is used to pump water for the irrigation of the trans-Volga steppes, where as much as 1,000,000 acres may be brought under cultivation.

Another asset of the Kuibyshev area is oil, which lies between the Volga and the Urals in great deposits, so productive that they are known as the Second Baku. These developments resulted in a doubling of the city's population during the two decades between the 1939 and 1959 census, so that it has come to be in the million category.

Volgagrad enjoys even greater advantages. Its dam produces more electricity than that at Kuibyshev, and it may draw on oil from either upstream or downstream. The Volga-Don Canal gives it access by water to the west, and enables coal and ore from the Ukraine to reach the north-south artery of the Volga. Although Volgagrad lacks near-by raw materials, it has become a great steel center. For thirty miles along the river is a succession of metallurgical works, tractor plants, lumber mills, shipyards, factories for making agricultural machinery, oil refineries, and general industry. It is well to remember, however, that the Volga is frozen for 150 days a year. Volgagrad marked the easternmost point of German advance during the Second World War; its defense by the Russians was one of the great battles of history.

Saratov, the third dam site along the lower river, is the traditional home of the Volga Germans, settled here under Catherine the Great.

Urals

The mineral wealth of the Urals has been known since the fifteenth century. The earliest developments yielded salt, silver, and gold; under Peter the Great, iron was smelted with the use of charcoal. By the nineteenth century, the region was also famous for its gems, semi-precious stones, and platinum.

Developments under socialist planning have been even more spectacular here than elsewhere. Great metallurgical plants have provided the base for diversified heavy industry. Mining now includes coal, oil, iron, copper, gold, platinum, silver, nickel, aluminum, manganese, asbestos, lead, zinc, magnesium, chromium, potash, salt, and ornamental building stones. No part of the Soviet Union is so richly mineralized; in fact, no mountain range on earth may be richer. Agriculture is of limited importance, but provides the materials for flour mills and leather tanning. The Urals form the country's second industrial base, next in importance to the Donets Basin.

Within the Ural region are numerous industrial cities. Sverdlovsk and Chelyabinsk are key centers for mining and manufacturing on the eastern side of the mountains. The former has a copper smelter, blast furnaces, and a large factory for heavy machinery, while the latter mines lignite, makes steel, and manufactures tractors. Sverdlovsk occupies a position with respect to the Urals which is somewhat comparable to that of Denver and the Rocky Mountains: both are supply and distributing centers for the near-by mining areas. Seven railway lines focus on the city. Perm and Ufa are old cities in the western hills, less affected by mining. Nizhni Tagil and Magnitogorsk are giant steel centers in the central mountains, with important railway car shops

at the former; the latter did not exist in 1929 but grew to 311,000 in
1959.

Railways cross the central Urals near Nizhni Tagil, Sverdlovsk, and
Chelyabinsk; and the southern Urals at Orsk and Aktiubinsk, with

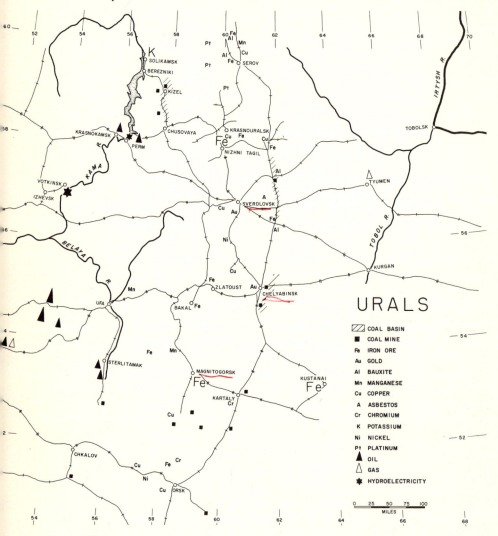

URALS

The Urals have the greatest variety of mineral production of any Soviet mountain range. Sverdlovsk, Chelyabinsk, and Magnitogorsk are giant industrial centers
based on near-by raw materials. While coal deposits are inferior, cheap energy is
available from oil fields to the west. Railway lines are shown with one or more
cross ties according to the number of their tracks.

another line west of Magnitogorsk. North-south lines parallel the mountains on either side.

The Urals are an old mountain range, worn down to rounded hills. In the north the structure continues to the islands of Novaya Zemlya, while in the south the Mogudjar Hills extend to the Aral Sea. As here considered, the Urals have an extent of 1,500 miles, with a maximum width of 325 miles in the latitude of Sverdlovsk.

On either side of the long and narrow central crystalline and metamorphic core are geosynclines of upper Paleozoic sedimentaries. Extensive folding and thrusting have complicated the structure. Volcanic intrusions accompanied the deformation and brought many of the ores. The major folding occurred in the Permian, after which the mountains were worn down to a peneplain and reuplifted in the Tertiary.

In terms of structure, the Urals have a threefold division. Along the east is a peneplained surface which bevels the folded sedimentaries and intrusives at elevations around 750 feet; in the center the crystalline core and intensely overthrust sedimentaries form the main mountain range; while the western section is a dissected plateau from 1,000 to 2,000 feet in elevation, developed on the gently folded rocks of the larger geosyncline. From north to south there is a fourfold division. The northern Urals are the highest and rise to 6,202 feet in Mt. Narodnaya. The central Urals are mere hills, under 1,000 feet where crossed by the railway opposite Sverdlovsk. Farther south, elevations reach 5,376 feet in Mt. Yoman-Tau. South of the Ural River the Mogudjar Hills lie at levels below 1,800 feet.

In geologic history and topography the Urals somewhat resemble the Appalachians. To the east of each range is a crystalline piedmont, to the west the hill lands of western Pennsylvania and eastern Ohio resemble the Ufa-Perm hills; both are dissected peneplains. In both the Urals and Appalachians, elevations reach a mile in the north and south, so that Mt. Narodnaya matches Mt. Washington, while Mt. Yoman-Tau corresponds to Mt. Mitchell. The major difference is that in Pennsylvania erosion has not as yet removed the sedimentary cover to expose the underlying metamorphic roots.

Climatic conditions are rigorous. Sverdlovsk has a July average of 63° F. and a January average of 3° F., with an annual rainfall of 22 inches. Higher elevations and west slopes receive more precipitation. Yearly averages at Sverdlovsk, Nizhni Tagil, Chelyabinsk, and Perm are all under 35° F. Average temperatures below freezing continue 170 days at Sverdlovsk, starting in mid October.

Vegetation zones grade from desert and steppe in the south through forest north of Magnitogorsk to tundra in the Arctic and on mountain summits. Where the forest has been cleared, the agricultural land is used for hay and pasture. Altitude reproduces latitude, for the same sequence is present from base to summit on the higher peaks.

If one might fly far enough to one side to see the entire range at once, the sequence of vegetation would be clear. Barren tundra covers

The Central Ural Mountains are low and rounded, crossed by several antecedent rivers. This is a view of the Trans-Siberian Express. (*Courtesy Soviet Union*)

the Arctic Urals. Farther south, with less rigorous climate, coniferous forests dominate. The Southern Urals extend into the dry steppe, and even reach the desert zone. Here, as elsewhere in the Soviet Union, it is the north-to-south contrasts in land usability which give variety to the landscape.

The Urals lack suitable metallurgical fuel. Charcoal was used originally, and lignite is available at Chelyabinsk. The Kizel bituminous coal is of inferior quality for coke but is so used in part. Oil is produced in the gentle folds to the west, and gas is found to the east; these have become major sources of fuel. There are few hydroelectric developments in the Urals, but power is available from dams along the Volga and the Kama.

Iron ore is the prime resource, with large deposits of magnetite near Nizhni Tagil, Zlatoust, Bakal, and Magnitogorsk. Blast furnaces of large dimensions operate at each city, as well as at Sverdlovsk and Chelyabinsk. Manganese is present, but is too high in phosphorus for satisfactory use. A long list of other minerals is in production. The Second World War brought a major expansion in mining, industry, and urban populations; most cities have doubled in size.

The problem of the metal industries in the Urals as elsewhere is that many deposits are of inferior quality or are remotely located with respect to fuel or markets. For example, the remaining ore at Magnitogorsk is poorer in iron and higher in sulphur than anticipated; elsewhere the ore is too titaniferous. The country urgently needs copper but, although the Urals have large smelters, the ore is of unsatisfactory quality. The same is true of aluminum. The significant fact is that despite all difficulties, socialist enthusiasm has achieved a noteworthy production. Some of these ores might not prove worth-while in a free economy, but in nationalistic terms their development has been justified.

Chapter VII

SOVIET MIDDLE ASIA

THE SECOND of the Union's three geographic provinces is Soviet Middle Asia, a land of rugged mountains and dry plains which extends across a million square miles of the U.S.S.R. from the Black Sea to the borders of China. In some ways this is the most colorful part of the country, both in landscape and in people. Picturesque non-Russian nationalities, many still wearing their traditional dress, live against a backdrop of snow-clad mountains, brown deserts, and green oases. Here history runs deep, and with an orientation southward to Iran and Turkey rather than toward the European and Mongol invasions which dominated Soviet Europe.

Soviet Middle Asia has not been a major producer, either in agriculture or industry. Arable land is limited, though expanding with irrigation, and the modest mineral production tends to supply factories elsewhere. Geological surveys suggest an important future for the metals and for coal, oil, and gas. The petroleum prospects are so promising that enthusiastic writers have referred to the area as a "Second Middle East," but such exuberance needs to await more detailed surveys.

In contrast to the closely spaced railway net and numerous navigable rivers of Soviet Europe, large areas of Middle Asia are a hundred miles from any modern means of transportation. There are almost no river boats, and few roads.

The rugged foothills of the Pamir Mountains in Middle Asia are the home of many non-Slavic peoples. This hunter with his falcon is a Kirgiz. Many of the people are nomads, moving up and down the slopes with the season. (*Tass*)

Five geographic regions are here described, one west of the Caspian Sea, the others to the east: Caucasia, the Caspian Desert, the Pamir Highlands, the Turan Oases, and the Aral-Balkhash Deserts.

Caucasia

Caucasia is a miniature world in itself. The region between the Black and Caspian seas comprises the alpine mountains and valleys from the Turkish-Iranian frontier north to the Kuban-Manych Plain. The mountains are geologically young but their human history is old, whereas with the Urals the reverse is true. Serving in some sense both as a bridge and a barrier to migration, this region has had a long and dramatic history. Across its passes were major trade routes known to

Each isolated valley in the Caucasus has its distinctive culture, in many cases with traditional animosities which make fortification desirable. The mountains have been both the cradle of the Caucasian "race," and a haven of refuge for minority peoples. (*Courtesy American Russian Institute*)

Assyrians and Romans. In the mountain valleys, cultures have been cradled and have found their graves.

Dozens of nationalities live in the region, many of them still wearing brightly colored native dress. These include Azerbaidzhanians, Georgians, Armenians, Russians, Ossetians, Abkhazians, Ajarians, Dagestani, Greeks, and Kurds. Bitter animosities have been the rule, with repeated persecution of minority peoples. This is the birthplace of Joseph Stalin, who was a Georgian.

Three union republics lie south of the main range, but the geographic region here considered also includes the north slopes of the Caucasus within the Russian Soviet Federated Socialist Republic. From west to east these three areas are the Georgian Soviet Socialist Republic, the Armenian S.S.R., and the Azerbaidzhan S.S.R. The entire area is about 80,000 square miles, only 1 per cent of the Union, while the population numbers 10,000,000, or some 5 per cent.

Caucasia includes three mountain ranges. The Greater Caucasus Mountains extend from the Caspian near Baku 685 miles northwest to the Black Sea beyond Novorossiisk, and the same structures reappear in Crimea. In the south the parallel Lesser Caucasus Range includes part of the high Armenian nucleus, largely in Turkey. Connecting these chains in the center are the low Suran Mountains. Between the main ranges are valleys that drain to the Black and Caspian seas. In the west is the Rion Valley and the Colchis lowland, while the east-flowing Kura River drains the Iberian lowland.

The Greater Caucasus Range is made up of folded sediments, with extensive igneous rocks toward the west. The highest mountain is volcanic Mt. Elbrus, 18,468 feet, which exceeds anything in Europe. Considerable areas are above the snow line, and there are about 1,400 glaciers. Serious earthquakes occur several times a century.

The connecting Suram Range is a granite mass which forms the watershed between the Rion and Kura rivers. There are passes as low as 3,280 feet.

The Lesser Caucasus is a block-faulted highland with numerous dormant volcanoes, generally from 6,000 to 10,000 feet high. Lake Sevan lies in the center. Just across the border in Turkey is volcanic Mt. Ararat, 16,916 feet.

Climate and vegetation vary abruptly with altitude and exposure. The Greater Caucasus Range stops cold northerly winds, while the Suram Range blocks moisture from the west. The Black Sea littoral has Mediterranean subtropical conditions, with 93 inches of rainfall at Batumi. The arid Caspian shore at Baku receives but 9 inches. Snow-

Snow crowns the higher Caucasus Range even in late summer. Some of the summits in this view north of Tbilisi reach 15,000 feet. (*G.B.C.*)

capped mountains are seen through palm trees, while deserts and swamps
are not far apart. The interior lowlands are similar to the northern
Balkans, and along the Black Sea conditions resemble the French
Riviera, whereas mountain climates resemble Novaya Zemlya. Deciduous forests cover the lower slopes, followed by conifers and meadows.
The flora is exceptionally rich, including 6,000 varieties of flowers. The
botanist Seifriz has remarked that "plants, like people, seemed to have
stopped here in their migratory journeys."

Agriculture is noted for the variety of subtropical products. Corn
is an old crop, but the area of cotton, grapes, tobacco, and fruits has
been greatly extended, and new crops have been added, such as tea,
citrus fruits, tung oil, cork oak, bamboo, and flax. The cultivated area
has been expanded by draining swamplands in the Colchis lowland and
by irrigation in the Iberian lowland. Wool and hides are produced in
the highlands. Tea production in western Georgia is almost sufficient

The western portions of subtropical Georgia produce most of the Union's tea. Ingenious tea-picking machines harvest the outer leaves. (*Courtesy U.S.S.R. National Committee, I.G.U.*)

to supply the entire Union. Caucasian wines have long been world-famous. Occasional frosts are a hazard.

Petroleum has been produced on the Apsheron Peninsula near Baku since 1869. In 1901, Baku supplied half the world output, and until the 1950's still accounted for one-half of Soviet production. Pipe lines lead to Batumi and to the Ukraine, but some of the oil is shipped by Caspian tankers to the Volga, so that Baku for decades was the first seaport of the entire U.S.S.R. Considerable oil is also produced along the northern foot of the Caucasus near Grozny and Maikop.

Manganese deposits at Chiatura are exceptionally large and high-grade. Ore is exported from Poti on the Black Sea.

Coal mines at Tkvarcheli and Tkibuli produce low-grade fuel. Hydroelectric possibilities are extensive, especially along the outlet from Lake Sevan. Small mining developments include copper, molybdenum, arsenic, and tungsten. Salt is obtained by evaporation from the Caspian. Mineral waters are bottled along the northern foothills.

Three cities are important, each the capital of its republic. Baku dominates Azerbaidzhan with a population of around a million, making it the fourth largest city of the Soviet Union; oil refining is the chief industry. Baku and much of the Trans-Caucasus area was once part of Persia, and the city did not pass into Russian hands until 1828. The city is located in a semi-desert, but irrigation provides for grass, flowers and palm trees. The name of the city reflects its adverse climate, for it comes from the Persian words, Bad-Kube, which refer to the strong north winds which bring clouds of dust. Near the city is a thirteenth-century Temple of the Fire Worshippers, built over ancient gas seeps.

Tbilisi, sometimes improperly spelled Tiflis, was founded fifteen centuries ago and owes some of its importance to its command of the principal highway across the central Caucasus which leads north to Ordzhonikidze. The city lies on the upper Kura River, and has become a center for light industry. Tbilisi is the capital of Georgia and has a population of nearly a million.

Yerevan is the center of Armenian culture, with a population of over half a million. The city lies in southernmost Transcaucasia, within sight of Mt. Ararat across the border in Turkey.

On the north slope of the Caucasus are the oil centers of Grozny and Maikop, and the industrial city of Krasnodar.

Southern Crimea is structurally a continuation of Caucasia, although its culture is more closely linked with that of the Ukraine. In southern Crimea the mountains descend abruptly to the Black Sea and protect the coast from cold northern winds. Although at latitude 45° N., the shore is a winter resort of some fame. Old czarist villas surround the city of Yalta.

Caspian Desert

The Caspian Sea occupies the lowest part of a vast area where no runoff reaches the ocean. If rainfall were more abundant or evaporation less, the basin would be filled to overflowing. During the more humid glacial period, the enlarged Caspian drained westward to the Black Sea with an outlet at an elevation of 150 feet, whereas the surface is now 85 feet below sea level.

Seventy per cent of the water intake of the Caspian comes from the Volga, and 19 per cent from direct precipitation. All of this is lost by evaporation. As climatic conditions vary, the level of the sea fluctuates. In the year 1306 the surface was 44 feet higher than at present, and in recent centuries there have been several changes, both up and down, with a range of 15 feet. During the first half of the twentieth century there was a drop of 6 feet. The increasing use of Volga water for irrigation will further lower the level. To balance this loss, it is proposed that part of the Amu Darya may be diverted through an ancient channel from near the Aral Sea to the Caspian, or that Arctic drainage may be turned to the headwaters of the Volga.

The Caspian level rises with cool wet summers along the Volga, whereas the Aral Sea level depends on melting snow in the Pamirs, with most runoff during hot dry summers.

Surrounding the Caspian Sea is a desert of limited usability. Much of it is covered with Quaternary sand and clay laid down by the expanded sea and reworked by the wind. Several depressions lie below sea level, one of them reaching –432 feet; since they receive no permanent streams, these basins are dry, or have only transitory salt lakes.

The Caspian Desert is invaded during the winter by cold air masses, so that temperatures drop to –22° F. in the Volga delta and the river is frozen for 112 days. During the summer, dry winds heated to 110° F. come from the east and blow with high velocity. These hot winds are known as *sukhovey*.

Rainfall is from 4 to 12 inches a year, as compared with annual evaporation from a free-water surface amounting to 48 to 60 inches, and from irrigated soil of 34 inches. Even the Volga and Ural diminish in size as they flow southward, while in winter the water of the Emba entirely evaporates before reaching the Caspian.

Agriculture is limited to irrigated strips along the rivers. A few nomads raise sheep and camels. Fishing is very important in the northern Caspian, especially for sturgeon and caviar.

Oil is produced from salt domes along the Emba River under conditions resembling the Texas and Louisiana Gulf Coast, and also east of the Caspian.

Borax and other minerals are secured from rich deposits at Inder Lake, where the production of borax compounds places the U.S.S.R. second to the United States in world output.

At the eastern side of the Caspian is Kara-Bogaz Gulf, enclosed except for a shallow entrance 400 feet wide. This bay receives no rivers, and evaporation is so great that the water contains 29 per cent of dissolved salts. Mirabilite, or sodium sulphate, is precipitated naturally and other chemicals are extracted. With the gradual lowering of the Caspian, the entrance to the Gulf has become dry and Caspian water no longer enters the bay. As a result, the water inside the barrier is rapidly evaporating.

The principal city of the region is Astrakhan, on a distributary of the Volga. The city has fish canneries and woodworking industries based on timber rafted down the Volga. Oil represents the major commerce, but extensive sand bars make it necessary for Caspian tankers to unload into barges well out from shore, and the oil is then transferred to river steamers at Astrakhan.

Pamir Highlands

Soviet territory reaches into the Pamirs and the great ranges that radiate from the roof of the world. Within the region are two of the Union's highest peaks, named Mt. Stalin, 24,584 feet in elevation, and Mt. Lenin, 22,377 feet. The second was originally thought to be the higher, and its name was changed from Kaufmann to Lenin, but corrected elevations showed the former Mt. Garbo to be of greater height and it was then renamed Mt. Stalin. The mountains form a continuous rampart between the Amu Darya and the Dzungarian Gate, a distance of a thousand miles.

The topography of the numerous ranges is complicated. The Pamirs are a mountainous plateau for the most part over 12,000 feet, with broad valleys five to ten miles wide cut by deep canyons and surrounded by rocky mountains. They lie between the Amu Darya and the Syr Darya.

The Tien Shan, or "heavenly mountains," so named from their extension into China, lie north of the Pamirs. Within the Soviet Union the range occupies the area between the Syr Darya and Ili River. The Tien Shan are a plateau, with mountain structures and once with mountain form but long ago reduced to old-age flatness and only recently re-uplifted. Erosion has thus been revived, especially around the margins.

The Pamir Region is the most active earthquake area in the Union, with many severe shocks.

Despite their distance from the sea, the higher Pamir areas receive from 20 to 80 inches of rain, some of it in the form of snow, and the highlands thus form the source of rivers which extend into and across the lowlands. These include the Amu and Syr Darya which enter the Aral Sea, and the Ili River which ends in Lake Balkhash. Enormous glaciers descend from the ranges, notably the 48-mile Fedchenko glacier near the Trans-Alai Range.

Precipitation in different areas ranges from arid to humid according to exposure; land use varies accordingly. The climate at lower elevations is generally dry, with long periods of clear weather. Forests are limited to favored exposures, with grass above and below. These upper and lower meadows are used for grazing sheep, horses, and cattle, with seasonal migration up and down the slopes. Lowland villages may be almost deserted during the summer while the flocks are on the upper slopes. While in the field, shepherds live in round, felt-covered kibitkas, similar to Mongolian yurts. Extensive upland areas are a cold desert, in contrast to the hot deserts of the lowlands.

Agriculture is restricted to the lower valleys and usually depends on irrigation. Many of the canals are very old. Climatic limitations on agriculture increase with altitude, as shown in the Zeravshan Valley, where rice is cultivated to 4,000 feet, corn to 4,300 feet, peaches to 4,500 feet, grapes to 5,900 feet, millet to 6,400 feet, apricots to 6,900 feet, and barley to 8,200 feet.

Two small republics lie in these mountains, the Kirgiz S.S.R., in the east, and the Tadzhik S.S.R. to the south. The capitals are Frunze and Dushanbe (formerly Stalinabad), each with about a quarter of a million population. Many of the people live in the bordering oases, to be considered in the following region.

Ancient caravan routes cross these mountains, though the passes are blocked by snow in winter. One famous route, followed by Marco Polo, leads over the Terek Pass to the Tarim Basin in China's western-

Rugged landforms limit land usability around the Pamir highlands. These folk dancers are in the Tadzhik Republic. (*Sovfoto*)

most province of Sinkiang, others go to Kashmir in northern India, and to Afghanistan. Two historic routes farther north connect the Lake Balkhash area with northwest China. One follows the Ili Valley, but the more famous and spectacular is through the Dzungarian Gate, a 46-mile gorge only 1,060 feet above sea level. Automobile roads now make the area more accessible, although some of these lead across passes above 10,000 feet.

Turan Oases

From the Caspian to the frontiers of China, and from the Pamirs to the borders of the agricultural land near the South Siberian Railway, lie a million square miles of arid and semi-arid lowland known as Turan. Much of it is uninhabitable desert except where mountain-nourished streams turn the waste into a garden. Within this area are two major landform divisions, the Turan Lowland in the south, and the Kazakh Upland farther north. In terms of land use there are two geographic regions: the Aral-Balkhash Deserts and the Turan Oases.

Three Union republics occupy this part of Soviet Middle Asia. The largest is the semi-arid Kazakh Soviet Socialist Republic, as large as all the rest of the Soviet Union excluding the Russian Republic. Parts of the Republic extend westward into the Caspian Desert and northward into the West Siberian Agricultural Region. Southeast of the Caspian Sea is the Turkmenian S.S.R., the driest, hottest and most desert of all the republics. Farther east is the Uzbek S.S.R., more developed than any of the republics east of the Caspian; here is one-third of the total population of Soviet Middle Asia, here is half of the industry, and here most of the Union's cotton is produced.

Since the recognized homeland of the Turkmenians is confined to the southwest corner of Turan, the name Turkestan cannot be applied to all of Soviet Middle Asia. Likewise the Kirgiz live in the mountains rather than in what has incorrectly been called the Kirgiz Steppe in Kazakhstan.

This is an ancient land of great individuality and unusual history. For thousands of years, the struggle against aridity has dominated all of life and has concentrated population in the few oases. Rainfall in most areas is quite inadequate for agriculture, so that cultivation depends upon irrigation from mountain streams fed by melting snow. Each river has its settlements in the midst of unreclaimed desert. These oases usually lie on the slopes of alluvial fans where the rivers leave the mountains, or extend along the flood plains as long ribbons running through the wilderness. Any geographic boundary of the Turan Oases which takes in all of these settlements must include much barren land. Economic characteristics appear more significant than cartographic continuity.

The oases here considered follow the foothills from Mari, once called Merv, in the west to Tashkent in the east. Other oases are so detached that they are best grouped with the desert region to follow. Mari is the chief settlement along the Murgab Valley, and one of the oldest cities of interior Asia. On the Amu Darya is Chardzhou, famed for the sweetness of its melons, with other towns upstream. Farther east is the historic Zeravshan Valley with the ancient cities of Bukhara and Samarkand.

The upper Syr Darya contains a large oasis in the Fergana Valley, almost surrounded by high mountains. The valley is 180 miles long by 100 miles wide, and supports half a dozen cities. This is one of the most densely populated areas in the U.S.S.R., with an elaborate irrigation system. Many irrigation canals are centuries old and have been considerably expanded by new engineering works, especially in areas where water is now brought to the dry side of the valley. Some of the ancient canals are fed by underground tunnels or horizontal wells known as karez or qanats, similar to those in Iran and Afghanistan.

After the snow-fed streams leave the mountains, they receive no tributaries and grow progressively smaller through seepage, evaporation, and diversion for irrigation. Most of the small streams that enter the Fergana Valley never reach the Syr Darya. Even the sizable Zeravshan withers in the desert without entering the Amu Darya. Although rainfall is at a minimum in summer, melting snow and glaciers make this the season of maximum flow.

The largest oases occupy alluvial fans between the mountains and the desert, at elevations from 1,000 to 1,500 feet above sea level. Rainfall is slightly higher than on the lowland plains and ground water more abundant, so that there may be a thin carpet of grass. As dust storms have swept across the desert through the centuries, silt has become trapped among this vegetation. This windborne dust is the loess, the basis of extremely fertile soils.

The continentality of the climate is shown in the fact that every station has a range between January and July means of over 50° F. July temperatures at Termez near Bukhara are the highest in the Union, with a maximum of 122° F. and a monthly average of 89.6° F. At Repetek, the sand temperature has reached 174° in July. Thanks to the dry air, most nights are cool. Winters are severely cold, with temperatures sometimes near those of Leningrad. Since the edge of invading

Siberian air masses is thin, cities on the plain may have lower temperatures than stations in near-by mountains. The snow cover is light, but persists for a month.

The precipitation is low and erratic. Tashkent averages 14 inches, which is considerably more than many stations. At Bukhara and Chardzhou the rainfall drops to 4 inches. Summer and fall are the driest seasons.

Large crops of cotton are grown on the irrigated lands of Middle Asia. This woman is a member of a collective farm in the Uzbek Republic. (*Tass*)

Cotton has been the chief crop since the American Civil War when decreased supplies gave Russia the impetus to produce her own needs. Cotton now occupies over half of the cultivated acreage. Wheat, rice, and barley are the chief grains. Increasingly, cotton textiles and some silk fabrics are woven in Middle Asia instead of being shipped in a raw state to the Moscow area. Sugar beets are important, since their sugar content is increased under conditions of desert irrigation. These oases have long been renowned for their fine fruit, such as apricots, peaches, cherries, plums, apples, melons, and grapes.

Although mining was not formerly significant, considerable development has taken place. The Fergana Valley contains fair coal. The nearby mountains have copper, lead, zinc, gold, silver, and arsenic. Hydroelectric power is used to develop phosphate fertilizers. Petroleum and natural gas were developed after the Second World War.

Ancient crafts included the weaving of carpets, preparation of fur and leather, metal work, pottery, and the manufacture of saddles; unfortunately, many of these arts have declined during recent decades. Keen rivalries between the wandering nomads and the sedentary oasis dwellers, as well as between rival oases, once brought raids and destruction. Each oasis has its own history.

Samarkand lies on the Zeravshan River, whose water is so valuable that the name means "gold spreading." The city's origin is unknown, but it has been "a sparkling jewel enticing the hearts of Kings through the ages." Alexander the Great plundered the city in 329 B.C. In the eighth century it was a center of Arab culture, and in the thirteenth century it was conquered by Genghis Khan. When Tamerlane made it his capital in 1370, he built the brilliantly decorated mosques, tombs, and other buildings that still stand. Surrounding the Registan square are the monumental buildings of three ancient colleges, each decorated with enameled tiles of turquoise blue. At the beginning of the eighteenth century, when there were almost no inhabitants, the city fell under Chinese control. Often destroyed by raiders from the deserts or mountains, Samarkand has been rebuilt many times. The history and ruins of Bukhara are equally impressive.

Tashkent lies in a large oasis on a tributary of the Syr Darya, the Chirchik. Tashkent developed at the intersection of historic trade routes, and is now the industrial metropolis of Soviet Middle Asia, with a wide array of machine and food industries, plus a steel mill. Its population is around a million.

Some of these oases were stepping stones along the ancient caravan route of Inner Asia. This highway from Peking to the Mediterranean followed the foot of the mountains from one river to another and was in use long before the days of Marco Polo. Along it flowed silk, porcelain, and art goods from China and India to Greece, Rome, and Roman Britain. At Samarkand, Bukhara, and Mari, merchants of the Orient met traders from the Occident.

The Oases of Southern Turan are inhabited by a wide variety of races, including people of ancient Iranian origin such as the Tajiks, and Turkic groups like the Kazakhs, Turkmens, Kirgiz, and Kara Kalpaks. Other groups include Arabs, Jews and Russians. The latter are

Timur the lame, or Tamerlane was born near Samarkand about 1336; after ruling the area from the Volga to the Ganges and the Great Wall of China, he was buried in this mausoleum. (*Tass*)

newcomers to this region, for Tashkent was not occupied by Russia until 1866 nor Bukhara till 1873.

This has long been a sensitive political area, and few outsiders have been able to travel freely. Even the 1914 Baedeker guidebook stated that "foreigners are not allowed to visit Turkestan except by special permission of the Russian Government. The traveler must send in his request . . . at the latest six months before the beginning of his journey."

Aral-Balkhash Deserts

Aridity dominates the Turanian plains. The annual precipitation averages only 8 inches, and in places is but half that figure. Where it reaches 12 inches in the north, some dry farming is attempted.

During the winter, when the region is exposed to cold Siberian air, the average January temperature drops well below freezing. The delta of the Amu Darya has recorded −14° F. In contrast to the imported winter weather, high summer temperatures are the result of local insolation. Day and night temperatures in July average 80 to 85° F., which is hotter than most areas within the tropics.

Many rivers enter the region, but only a few have enough water to penetrate very far into the desert; those which persist end in salt lakes or playas. Whereas normal rivers in humid lands gain water from tributaries and flow *in* valleys which they are eroding, these desert streams lose water, become overloaded with sediment, and flow *above* their flood plain. Sand bars and shifting channels make navigation difficult or impossible.

Although northern Kazakhstan has over 5,000 small lakes, many of them are ephemeral. The major water bodies are the Aral Sea and Lake Balkhash, both properly to be termed "seas" since they lack an outlet. The former stands next to the Caspian as the second largest inland body of water in the Old World. A large part is only 30 to 60 feet deep, and the area fluctuates. Western Lake Balkhash is freshened by waters of the Ili River, while the eastern portion of the lake is salty from evaporation.

Within the region are several subregions where variations in geology, altitude, or climate introduce minor differences. The Kara Kum and Kizil Kum are sandy deserts on either side of the Amu Darya. Some of the shifting sand areas may be due to the destruction of sparse natural vegetation by overgrazing or attempted cultivation. East of the Syr Darya is the Golodnaya Steppe, slightly higher and a bit more moist. The Bedpak Dala or Hunger Steppe lies north of the Chu River, while on the south shore of Lake Balkhash is the Semireche Steppe. In the north, the Kazakh Hills are a peneplained mountain range, often incorrectly termed the Kirgiz Steppe.

The soil is generally unleached serozem, a gray desert soil, with local salty or alkaline areas where ground water is close enough to the sur-

The rolling Kazakh hills with their short grass provide extensive grazing lands for sheep, cattle, and horses. These animals belong to a collective farm. (*Tass*)

face to permit evaporation of capillary moisture. The most prominent vegetation is desert brush.

Most of the people in the region live in oases, similar to those described in the previous section on the Turan Oases. Former nomads have now been collectivized. Hides, wool, meat, and grain are important products. Astrakhan sheep are raised in the south.

The Kazakh Hills, in part the roots of an ancient mountain range, are richly mineralized, and appear to contain half of the Union's copper, lead, zinc, and nickel. In their rich mineralization the Kazakh Hills resemble the Urals. Karaganda is one of the major producers of coal, some of which supplies the steel industry in the Urals. Near the northern shore of Lake Balkhash is a great copper mine at Kounrad, with another development to the west at Djezkazgan. Sulphur is obtained north of Ashkhabad, and lead at Chimkent near Tashkent.

The chief cities outside the semicontinuous belt of oases are Ashkhabad in the southwest, capital of the Turkmenian S.S.R.; Frunze and

Alma Ata, capitals of the Kirgiz and Kazakh republics, respectively; Kounrad and its near-by copper smelters at Balkhash; and the coal city of Karaganda.

Mechanized agriculture has brought large areas of semi-arid land into cultivation. These combines are on a state farm in Kazakhstan. (*Photo by I. Budnevich*)

Chapter VIII

SIBERIA

SIBERIA IS not a political entity, but a geographical expression for the eastern two-thirds of the Soviet Union. Here live thirty million people, in a still-expanding economy. This is one of the last great pioneering lands on earth. Siberia has many different landscapes. The Arctic tundra, the wooded taiga, and the dry steppe each spread over vast areas. Desert areas are essentially absent, present instead in Soviet Middle Asia to the southwest and in Mongolia to the southeast. Siberian agriculture occupies a thin, tapering zone along the Trans-Siberian Railway.

Inaccessibility has long presented a problem. The main railroads and their branches serve only a small fraction of the area. Vast areas in the taiga are almost inaccessible due to swamps and fallen timber, but across the southern steppes one may travel on horseback or by car across country. Rivers provide avenues for boats in summer and frozen highways in winter. Transport is no longer limited to north-flowing rivers, or to a single railway. The Trans-Siberian is double-tracked throughout, and the total railway mileage east of the Urals has tripled since czarist days. Airplane service has revolutionized access to many urban areas.

Since the broad plains of Siberia have no exposed rock, it is only near the mountains or rivers that crushed stone or river gravel is avail-

---

The Siberian taiga is one of the world's largest forests. Excellent commercial timber is found toward the south; farther north trees are stunted. Hunters find an abundance of fur-bearing animals. (*Tass*)

able for highways or railroads. Elsewhere, many Siberian roads are merely a set of cart ruts which meander across the country. Where one pair of ruts becomes too deep, another track is started alongside. Roads may thus be several hundred yards wide. Across the central part of the country, from the Ural Mountains to the Pacific Ocean, runs the Great Siberian Track. Very little of it is a properly paved road, and the best is a gravel highway over which trucks seldom exceed thirty miles an hour.

This is one of the few remaining areas of pioneering agriculture outside the tropics, and into it the Russian farmers have gone by the millions. Some of the thrill which characterizes Soviet developments is associated with the cultivation of virgin land. The environment places many restrictions on agriculture, but the potentials are still considerable. Since the revolution the area of cultivated land has more than tripled. Urban developments are also spectacular, including a dozen Siberian cities with a population between 100,000 and 1,000,000.

Siberia is proving to be a great storehouse of mineral and agricultural

The great dam at Bratsk on the Angara River has led to the development of this new city in the midst of the Siberian taiga. (*Courtesy Soviet Embassy, Washington*)

wealth. While the total possibilities are impressive, it is well to keep
a perspective in terms of accessibility, quality, and markets. This is a
huge area, and the development of these resources will require vast
amounts of capital and decades of time.

Within Siberia are five million square miles of plains and mountains,
of taiga and steppe. Here is the world's greatest forest, and here are
four of the world's longest rivers. Ten geographic regions may be
recognized, as follows: the West Siberian Agricultural Region; the
Altai-Sayan Mountains; the Ob Taiga; the Yenisei Taiga; the Arctic

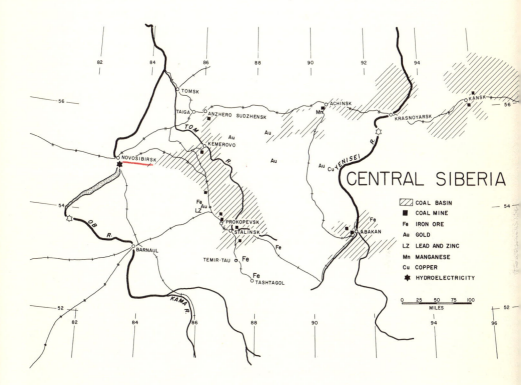

CENTRAL SIBERIA

The Kuznetsk Basin along the Tom River has become the Union's great eastern
center for heavy industry. There are vast reserves of high grade coal, both here
and near the Yenisei, but the local iron ore is of inferior quality. Novosibirsk and
Krasnoyarsk are the main cities on the double-tracked Trans-Siberian Railway.
The single-track South Siberian Railway connects Novo Kuznetsk and Barnaul
with the southern Urals.

Fringe; Baikalia; the Lena Taiga; the Northeastern Mountains; the Far East; and Sakhalin and the Kuriles.

West Siberian Agricultural Region

The surveyors who laid out the Trans-Siberian Railway toward the close of the nineteenth century proved to be practical geographers, for they placed it along what has become the eastward continuation of the agricultural triangle. The railway alternately runs through rich grasslands and the coniferous forest.

The colonization of Siberia dates from the seventeenth century. Some of the first travelers followed the rivers, portaging from the tributary of one north-flowing river to a tributary of the next. Early settlers kept within the uninhabited forest or along the northern edge of the steppe to avoid conflict with nomadic Mongol tribes farther south.

The West Siberian Agricultural Region is one of the flattest areas on earth. Along the main railway one travels 1,200 miles from the Urals to the Yenisei, scarcely seeing a hill. From Omsk to Novosibirsk the railway gradient in most places is only four inches per mile. Much of the area is covered with unconsolidated Quaternary continental deposits, beneath which are Tertiary marine sediments. Vast glacial lakes, dammed by ice sheets which once blocked drainage to the Arctic, left sediments that add to the flatness. Even the folded lands of the Kazakh Hills have been worn down to low relief and gentle slopes. In the steppeland south of the railway are countless thousands of shallow depressions, sometimes filled with transitory lakes, which apparently represent wind-scour during a period of greater aridity and less vegetation.

Wide seasonal variations characterize the temperature. Total winter snowfall is light, but occasional blizzards pile the snow into formidable drifts that may disrupt railway traffic. Half the year has freezing temperatures, for the average falls below that point in mid-October, to remain until mid-April. The short summers have several days that are uncomfortably warm, but average temperatures exceed 68° F. for only a month. Precipitation is from 12 to 18 inches, chiefly in the summer.

This is the Asiatic combination and continuation of two geographic areas west of the Urals, the Central Agricultural Region of cleared forest with podsol soils, and the Southern Agricultural Region of cultivated steppe underlain by chernozem soils. Both landscapes are present in western Siberia, although most agricultural development has taken place in the steppe where there are no forests to be cleared and soils

Vast areas of Siberia are covered with the trackless coniferous forest known as the taiga, a seemingly inexhaustible source of timber and of furs. (*Courtesy Soviet Embassy, Washington*)

are more fertile. This is the tapering end of the triangle, pinched between limitations of cold on the north and drought on the south, and limited eastward by unfavorable topography in the Altai, Sayan, and Baikal mountains.

The great crop of the region is spring wheat, with large amounts of oats, rye, and barley. Huge grain elevators rise at every railway station and can be seen across the plain long before the town comes in sight. Flour milling is a major industry. This part of Siberia is an important cattle country, long famous for its export of butter and hides. Meat packing is significant. As a result, the West Siberian Agricultural Region is an area of food surplus, with large shipments to other regions.

Along the southern margins of the agricultural triangle, several million acres of virgin steppe were brought under cultivation during the late 1950's. Nomadism has been replaced by agriculture. Crops are good in years of adequate rainfall, but fail when drought occurs or frosts come too early.

The Kazakh Republic contains vast areas of virgin land, unplowed until the mid-twentieth century. While they are underlain by fertile chestnut brown soils, the rainfall is limited and variable. (*Tass*)

Russian villages have surprisingly little in the way of commercial activities. Even settlements of several hundred houses have no store, for people live a nearly self-sufficient existence. Log houses are the rule in the north, replaced by sod houses where timber is not available. Each house has a huge brick stove which occupies nearly a quarter of the kitchen and which often has a platform on top where some of the family may sleep during the winter. Behind each house is usually a vegetable plot, with a barn for the farmer's own cow, pigs, and chickens. The rest of the cultivated land is collectivized and worked co-operatively.

Most of Soviet Siberia has a twofold economic pattern. The rivers provide a north-south orientation, while the Trans-Siberian Railway is an east-west integrator. The West Siberian Agricultural Region is dominated by the railway, while the geographic regions of the Ob, Yenisei, and Lena taiga, to be described later, are river-oriented.

Where rail and water meet, significant cities develop. Since the Irtysh, Ob, and Yenisei are the major rivers which intersect the Trans-Siberian Railway, their crossings at Omsk, Novosibirsk, and Krasnoyarsk, respectively, are the leading cities. The city of Tomsk on the Tom, an Ob tributary, is one of the oldest centers in Siberia, but has grown more slowly than the others since it is on a branch railway. Upstream from Novosibirsk on the Ob is the agricultural center of Barnaul. Industrialization and urban modernization generally decrease with distance from Moscow, and with the size of the river.

The largest Siberian city is Novosibirsk, a thousand miles east of the Urals, with a population of nearly a million people. This industrial center lies just to one side of the Kuznetsk Basin, to which it is parasitic in somewhat the same way that Ukrainian Kharkov is to the Donets Basin. Banks, department stores, and an opera house seating 5,000 people face the central square.

At these latitudes all rivers tend to be deflected to their right by the rotation of the earth; accordingly the eastern bank is often undercut and high, while the other is low and swampy. Approaching Siberian rivers from the west, one typically finds a broad swampy flood plain, miles in width, which the railway crosses on an embankment rising to 50 feet or more in height. Then the river is crossed by a bridge and the train at once enters a city on the high right bank.

Altai-Sayan Mountains

South central Siberia is bordered by a continuation of the young mountains which appear in the Caucasus, continue through the Pamirs and Tien Shan, and extend across China to reach the Pacific. The Altai and Sayan ranges extend for a thousand miles from the Dzungarian Gate in Soviet Middle Asia to near Lake Baikal. On a purely geologic basis, half the mountain area lies in Mongolia, but no geographically meaningful region can ignore a political boundary such as that of the Soviets.

The region is mountainous but is geographically important for its mineral wealth rather than its topography. Here is a large share of the country's best coal. Deposits of lead, zinc, silver, gold, copper, tin, and manganese are significant. Waterpower developments along the upper Irtysh, Ob, and Yenisei are impressive. Although much of the area was once somewhat difficult of access, railway lines lead southward into the mining areas of Ridder, Kuznetsk, and Minusinsk.

Both the Altai and the Sayan were folded in the middle and late Paleozoic and then, after being worn down to essential peneplains, were

The coal fields of the Kuznetsk Basin may contain as much as a trillion tons of coal. This is a view of the modern colliery at Prokopevsk. (*Courtesy Soviet Embassy, Washington*)

again uplifted during the late Tertiary. The central portions of the mountains remain rolling uplands above 10,000 feet, comparable to the Pamirs and the Tien Shan, with active dissection on the margins.

The Altai system has a general northwest-southeast trend, which continues far into Mongolia. Several divisions may be distinguished within the Soviet Union. The Tarbagatai Range lies between the Dzungarian Gate and Lake Zaisan on the Irtysh. Between the Irtysh and Ob are the Altai Mountains proper, culminating in Mt. Belukha, 15,154 feet. Six glaciers radiate from this peak, descending to an elevation of 6,400 feet; one of them is five miles long. The snow line is from 8,000 to 10,000 feet. East of the Ob lie the Eastern Altai, reaching almost to the Yenisei and formed of two north-south ranges, the Salair and the Kuznetsk-Alatau, respectively west and east of the Kuznetsk Basin.

The two ranges of the Sayan system surround the Minusinsk Basin. The Eastern Sayan, with elevations up to 11,447 feet, is the main range, extending from Lake Baikal to the Yenisei, with a southern branch known as the Western Sayan. Neither the Kuznetsk nor the Minusinsk basins are level, and the railways need long, steep grades to climb the rolling hills.

The Tanna Tuva Basin occupies the headwaters of the Yenisei, encircled by the Western Sayan and the Tannu Ola. This area was formerly a part of China, but has long been claimed by the U.S.S.R., since it lies within the Yenisei Basin. It was unilaterally annexed in 1946.

Rainfall at the foot of the mountains and in the interior basins does not exceed 10 inches but increases notably on the upper slopes. In the Western Sayans at 3,840 feet, the Olenya Creek station receives 47 inches, while in the Western Altai, the Andobin Mine with an elevation of 1,800 feet has 37 inches. Summer is the rainy season, and the distant Atlantic is the apparent source of the moisture.

Winter temperature inversions, combined with the thinness of the Siberian cold air masses, make the highlands a relatively warm island between the cold plains of Siberia and Middle Asia. On the other hand, interior valleys such as the Minusinsk Basin receive cold air drainage from the surrounding mountains. Minusinsk has a January average of –5° F., and an extreme low of –65.7° F. Both temperatures are lower than anywhere farther north along the Yenisei River, even near the Arctic Ocean. July temperatures at Minusinsk average 69° F.

Steppe vegetation covers the lower slopes of the Altai-Sayan Mountains up to some 3,000 feet, above which there is a splendid forest of Siberian larch, cedar, fir, pine, and birch to 6,000 feet or more, followed by alpine meadows to the snow line around 9,000 feet.

As the steppe grass is usually too short to be harvested, and native agriculture is impractical, the original inhabitants were nomads. These former pastoralists now live in collectivized villages. Along the upper Tom and Yenisei rivers one-quarter of the lowland has been cultivated by modern methods and is now in wheat, potatoes, and sunflower. Large areas of steppe have been plowed in the Minusinsk Basin. The chernozem soil is attractive but, with the breaking of the sod, dust-bowl conditions are apt to develop in drier years.

Coal is the great mineral resource, with reserves of at least a trillion metric tons in the Kansk-Achinsk and Kuznetsk basins, and smaller amounts in the Minusinsk Basin. The Cheremkhovo mines west of Irkutsk also have large reserves.

The key location in mineral development east of the Urals is Kuznetsk, where there are fabulous reserves of high-grade coal. The Kuznetsk Basin lies near Novosibirsk a hundred miles south of the Trans-Siberian Railway. There are half a dozen coal-mining centers, with single mines which produce many millions of tons of coal a year.

The Kuznetsk Basin is a closely folded syncline, with many beds dipping 60° to 80°. The carbon ratio of the coal is from 80 to 89 per cent, with sulphur at 0.5 per cent. Much of the coal is of coking quality, and some is suitable for gas and chemical use. Production amounted to 774,000 metric tons in 1913, rose to 16,800,000 tons in 1938, and in 1956 reached 66,200,000 tons, one-seventh of the national total. The chief mining centers are Novo Kuznetsk (formerly Stalinsk), Prokopyevsk, Leninsk-Kuznetsk, Kemerovo, and Anzhero-Sudzhensk.

Surrounding the Kuznetsk Coal Basin are several metal mines. Zinc, gold, and lead are obtained at Salair. Great amounts of iron ore are mined in the Gornaya Shoria Range to the south; the iron content is good but the high sulphur must be removed before smelting. The city of Novo Kuznetsk has some of the largest iron and steel furnaces in the Union. Eastward across the mountains in the Minusinsk Basin is excellent iron ore southwest of Abakan, which some day may be developed with near-by coal.

In the Altai at Ridder, southeast of Barnaul, are large lead and zinc plants. This area, among the country's oldest mining districts, also yields silver, gold, copper, and tin. Prehistoric people used bronze tools in their mining operations here.

Manganese occurs near Achinsk, but the ore contains only 20 to 25 per cent manganese in comparison with 50 per cent at Chiatury and 40 per cent at Nikopol.

Cities with smoking factories rise in the Kuznetsk Basin as abrupt and exotic intrusions in a treeless land scarcely inhabited even by nomads before the First World War. Centers such as Novo Kuznetsk, Prokopyevsk, and Kemerovo give the Kuznetsk area an urban population of nearly a million.

The development of great steel works and associated industries in the midst of the empty Kuznetsk steppe is one of the major achievements of the Soviet Union. Whereas Kuznetsk was originally dependent on Ural iron ore 1,200 miles to the west, local resources are now nearly sufficient. Their quality is lower, but the saving in transport is obvious.

Ob Taiga

The flatness of the West Siberian Plain is shown in the gradient of the Ob River. At Novosibirsk, 1,850 miles from its mouth, the elevation is 308 feet, a slope of only two inches per mile. Although the West

Siberian Plain continues from the Urals eastward beyond the Yenisei to the edge of the Central Siberian Uplands, the geographic region here considered ends near the left bank of the Yenisei. The Ob was the first Siberian river to be developed and still has better steamers and more freight than the others.

The Ob has a length of 3,200 miles, and is joined by the Irtysh, which in turn receives the Ishim and Tobol. The length of rivers navigable at high water in the Ob system totals 19,000 miles. Nearly half the freight, chiefly grain and timber, is carried on the Irtysh, navigable upstream into China. The river is blocked by ice 190 days at Tobolsk, and for 210 days at Salekhard near the gulf. Near Tobolsk, winter ice is 30 to 40 inches thick; at Salekhard 40 to 60 inches.

The Ob Taiga as a geographic entity lies north of the croplands of the West Siberian Agricultural Region. The region has a typical boreal climate, DC in Koeppen symbols. Winters are long and accumulate a considerable snow cover. The annual precipitation is about 18 inches, decreasing to 14 inches near the Arctic.

The coniferous forest resembles that of the Dvina-Pechora Taiga in general, but lower rainfall, a more severe winter, and poor drainage change many species. Siberian fir predominates, mixed with white-barked trees such as birch and aspen. The Vasyugan Swamp covers 100,000 square miles near the junction of the Ob and Irtysh. Timber is shipped from Salekhard, usually consigned to Arkhangelsk rather than exported abroad. Very large amounts move upstream to the Trans-Siberian Railway for urban and industrial needs.

There are few cities of significance, and many place names shown on maps are riverside clearings of a few dozen houses. Large areas are completely without settlement, inaccessible in summer because of swamps and mosquitoes. Contact with the rest of the Union is chiefly through cities to the south where the railway taps the Ob, Irtysh, or other tributaries.

Yenisei Taiga

From the source of the Yenisei to the ocean is 2,619 miles, but if the distance be measured along its major tributary, the Angara, and its extensions beyond Lake Baikal, the length is 3,553 miles. Fourth among the world's rivers in length, the Yenisei ranks seventh in drainage area with over a million square miles. The river lies at the latitude of the Mackenzie in Canada, placing Krasnoyarsk on the same parallel as Edmonton, and Igarka at the same distance beyond the Arctic Circle as Aklavik.

Most of the Yenisei Taiga is within the Central Siberian Upland, particularly in the Tunguska Hills which gradually rise to an elevation of 4,500 feet along the Lena divide. From these uplands the Yenisei receives three major tributaries. In the south the Verkhne or Upper Tunguska, commonly called the Angara, flows out of Lake Baikal. In the middle is the Podkamena or Stony Tunguska, while the northern tributary is the Nizhni or Lower Tunguska.

Virgin forest extends from south of the Angara 750 miles northward to beyond Igarka. This taiga is a trackless expanse of conifers and whitewoods. Toward the south, and especially along the Angara, are splendid stands of commercial pine, but adverse climate in the north reduces the trees to less than a foot in diameter. These forests are so vast that only preliminary studies as to the commercial reserves have been possible.

The taiga is usually described as a coniferous forest of fir, pine, and larch, but airplane flights along the Yenisei reveal that birch and deciduous trees cover a third of some areas.

Sawmills are in operation at Krasnoyarsk, Yeniseisk, and Igarka, with a large overseas export from the latter city, largely to Western Europe.

Permanently frozen ground underlies almost the entire region. Summer warmth thaws the ground to a depth of two or three feet beneath the insulating forest, or as deep as ten feet on cleared ground. Below these depths temperatures below freezing prevail to a thousand feet and more.

The Tunguska Hills contain enormous reserves of coal, known along the rivers and thought to continue between them. Tentative estimates reach hundreds of billions of tons. Igneous intrusions of trap rock have locally altered the coal to graphite, mined since 1862.

The Yenisei is the great unifier of the region, for most settlement is along its waterways. Several dozen freight and passenger boats operate on the river. Regular steamboat lines lead from the railway at Krasnoyarsk; going south in three days to Minusinsk, north in six days to Igarka, and in two days more to Dudinka. Through most of the region the river is over a mile in width; depths exceed 50 feet except in the estuary where there are numerous sand bars.

The first Russians reached the lower Yenisei via the Arctic in 1610, whereas overland travelers from Tomsk did not see the river until Yeniseisk was established in 1618.

One of the most interesting cities of the Yenisei Taiga is the seaport of Igarka, which provides a sheltered anchorage where cargoes can be transferred between river and ocean vessels. Although within the Arctic Circle, it lies 400 miles inland from the shallow and stormy estuary. In

1929 Igarka was a settlement with one house and three people; by 1937 its population numbered 15,000. The largest lumber mills east of the Urals cut logs floated down from the Angara for shipment during the two-month navigation period in August and September when the Kara Sea is open. To keep people healthy, fresh vegetables are raised in greenhouses and on open fields. Root crops do well, and leafy vegetables are reasonably successful, but grain usually does not ripen. Several hundred cows supply fresh dairy products and the animal manure which is essential if crops are to grow.

The great city of the region is the river-rail junction of Krasnoyarsk, but it is placed with the West Siberian Agricultural Region rather than the Yenisei Taiga.

Arctic Fringe

Although the Arctic may not appear to be the most attractive part of the Soviet Union, there are few other regions whose development has met with equal enthusiasm. Nearly half the arctic lands of the earth lie within the U.S.S.R., and no other country has given so much attention to the development of northern latitudes. The Northern Sea Route Administration is a modern Hudson's Bay Company. To it is entrusted Arctic navigation and the economic development of all the north.

Interest in northern Sibera and a possible northeast passage to China dates from the middle of the sixteenth century when the Spanish and Portuguese dominated the route around Africa so that the Dutch and English tried to sail via the north of Asia. Sebastian Cabot sent out an expedition in 1553 with instructions to "use all wayes and meanes possible to learn how men may passe from Russia either by land or by sea to Cathaia." Henry Hudson was another who explored this route, but neither expedition was able to sail east of Novaya Zemlya.

Russian merchant adventurers later sailed to the mouth of the Ob and founded a trading post in 1608, but the fear of foreign penetration led the czar to forbid all Arctic navigation in 1624. Modern commerce reached the Yenisei again under Nordenskjöld in 1875, and in 1878–79 he made the first voyage to the Pacific. During the Russo-Japanese War of 1904–05, 22 ships were sent to the mouth of the Yenisei to relieve traffic on the railway.

Soviet activities on an extensive scale date from 1932 when the ice-breaker *Sibiriakov* made the first voyage from Arkhangelsk to Vladivostok in a single season. Under the Northern Sea Route Administration, regular services now operate to the mouths of the various rivers and many vessels make the complete transit each summer. Icebreakers and scouting airplanes are used in the most difficult areas. Service to the Kolyma River and points eastward is usually routed via Vladivostok; Arkhangelsk is the main port for supplying the western area, including the Lena. Except for exports of Yenisei lumber, most goods are consigned inward. During the Second World War, large quantities of supplies were shipped from Portland, Oregon, via Bering Strait to ports in the Soviet Arctic.

Four groups of islands divide the Soviet Arctic into five seas. The chief ports of the Barents Sea are Murmansk and Arkhangelsk. Ice forms early in October, reaching its maximum thickness and extent at the end of April. The Murmansk coast remains ice-free owing to the warm Atlantic drift. To the east of the Barents Sea are the two islands of Novaya Zemlya, or new land, separated by the narrow Matochkin Strait, ice-free for 4 months but fog-bound for 19 days each month in summer. Alternate passages lead north or south of the islands.

East of Novaya Zemlya lies the Kara Sea, bounded on the east by Severnaya Zemlya, or north land. Ice forms a month earlier and persists a month longer than in the Barents Sea. Both the Ob and the Yenisei have broad estuaries with sand bars where the depth of water is 16 and 23 feet, respectively. On the Ob, the chief river port is the rail terminus of Salekhard, but most ocean vessels must unload at Novi Port in the estuary, where there is a floating wharf 2 miles from the shore. At the mouth of the Yenisei, barren Dickson Island has a good harbor but cannot be reached by river boats, so that transshipment takes place at Igarka, 400 miles up river, or at Dudinka which is the port for the railway which leads 50 miles east to the mining city of Norilsk.

The Laptev or Nordenskjöld Sea occupies the section from Severnaya Zemlya to the New Siberian Islands. Its chief port is Tiksi on the edge of the Lena delta, but at one side of the river, since a ten-foot sand bar blocks ocean vessels from the Lena itself. Shipping also calls at Nordvik on the Khatanga River where there is a small production of salt and petroleum.

The East Siberian Sea, beyond the New Siberian Islands, is so shallow that navigation is difficult. Sand bars at the mouths of the Kolyma and Indigirka rivers necessitate transshipment in the open sea. On the east the sea terminates at Wrangel Island, around which ice conditions are the worst of the entire passage. The Chuckchee Sea continues to Bering Strait.

To supplement the steamer services, an air line operates from Moscow to Arkhangelsk, Igarka, Tiksi, and the Chukotski Peninsula, 4,500 miles distant.

Even though the navigation period is short and the hazards considerable, there is strategic value in a protected route from Murmansk to Vladivostok. The naval significance is suggested by the fact that in the war with Japan in 1905 the Russian fleet was obliged to sail around Africa and arrived in Japanese waters quite unprepared for combat. Like the United States of America, the Union of Soviet Socialist Republics is a two-ocean country, and the Northern Sea Route in a sense has become Russia's Panama Canal.

The Soviet Union claims ownership of all land in the sector north of the U.S.S.R. to the Pole. In 1937–38, a scientific station occupied the North Pole, where the ocean depth was found to be 14,075 feet.

Wandering hunters and fishermen spend the summers in birchbark wigwams along the streams where they catch and dry fish, while the winter months are devoted to trapping. Many people raise reindeer.

Many of the people in the Arctic trap for furs in winter and spend their summers catching fish from the rivers. These Evenki have pitched their birchbark wigwam along the northern Yenisei. (*G.B.C.*)

Several Mongol peoples are represented, some of them similar to nomads who also keep reindeer in the Sayan Mountains near the headwaters of the Yenisei. The names Samoyed and Tungus were once used for groups who should now be termed Nentsi and Evenki. Formerly without a written language, they have been given an alphabet. Schools, medical centers, and reindeer-breeding stations have been provided. Other people are the Chuckchee, Koryaks, and Yakuts.

Surface travel across the tundra is difficult during the brief summer, for there are innumerable swamps and lakes. According to a native saying, "there are as many lakes as there are stars in the sky." Some of these resulted from unequal deposition of glacial drift; others are related to uneven melting in the permanently frozen ground.

Normal agriculture is almost impossible, but every commercial and scientific outpost has experimental gardens and greenhouses. On Dickson Island electricity generated by the wind is used to light and heat underground greenhouses.

Conditions near the southern margin of the tundra are illustrated by Dudinka, an old settlement of 3,000 and the administrative and commercial center for the Taimyr Okrug. Each year's fur catch is valued at several million rubles, and a few tons of ivory from ice-age mammoths are shipped annually. The frost-free period averages less than 60 days. The temperature dropped to –42° F. on Feb. 28, 1937, and the monthly average was –9° F. Every month has from 64 to 87 per cent cloudiness. Precipitation amounts to 9 inches, almost entirely in the late summer.

Baikalia

Lake Baikal is 400 miles long and imposes a barrier to all east-west travel across southern Siberia. High mountains along the near-by Mongolian frontier force the railway to follow a corridor around the lake. Farther north the Stanovoi Mountains continue to the Lena Valley. When approaching Baikalia from the west, the Yenisei Ridge and the Eastern Sayan Mountains restrict travel to the Krasnoyarsk gateway, so that the only feasible route is by way of the Angara and Irkutsk.

The geographic region of Baikalia lies largely to the east of the lake. Confused mountain structures trend northeast-southwest, and include the Pre-Baikal, Trans-Baikal, Yablonovi, and Olekminsk-Stanovik ranges. Much of the region is formed of crystalline and metamorphic rocks, with elevations over a mile.

The lake occupies a graben that makes it the deepest lake in the world, 5,314 feet (1960). Surrounding mountains are 6,600 feet high, so that the fault displacement is more than two miles. Occasional severe earthquakes indicate the sensitive nature of the geology. In area, Lake Baikal is in seventh place among the world's lakes, but in volume it ranks second. The Selenga is the chief of its tributaries, while the Angara forms the only outlet.

Because of the volume of Lake Baikal, the maximum temperature of the surface water is delayed until August, and freezing does not occur until January. As a result, the shores have only 90 days below 14° F., while there are 140 such days near by. In summer, the immediate vicinity of Baikal has only 70 days with an average of 50° or over, as compared with 100 such days elsewhere. Fishing is important. The climate of Baikalia as a whole appears to represent the furthermost penetration of summer monsoon winds from the Pacific.

Most of Baikalia is covered by a pine forest, with Mongolian-type steppe in the drier lowlands. Cultivated land totals several million acres. Many of the rural people are Buriat Mongols, who specialize in cattle raising. Russians dominate the cities. Fishing is important.

Tremendous hydroelectric developments along the Angara, notably the great Bratsk Dam and that at Irkutsk, are in the process of making this one of the major industrial centers of the U.S.S.R. Coal is mined both east and west of the lake, and iron is produced in a plant at Petrovsk. The region also has numerous occurrences of tin, tungsten, zinc, gold, arsenic, and molybdenum.

The Trans-Siberian Railway links the three major cities. Irkutsk lies on the Angara, 44 miles west of Lake Baikal, and is the leading city of east-central Siberia. Ulan-Ude lies at the rail crossing of the Selenga and is the junction for the railway south to the Mongolian People's Republic, and Peking. The city has a large meat-packing plant. Chita lies near the railway junction to Manchuria.

Lena Taiga

Two features of the Lena Valley are of special interest: gold production and the new railway to the Lena River north of Lake Baikal.

Gold has been obtained from the rivers of the northeast for many decades, and early in the twentieth century was exploited by a large British concession named Lena Goldfields. Production greatly expanded with the discovery of the Aldan fields in 1923 where placer and lode deposits contribute much of the country's gold. An automobile road leads south to the Trans-Siberian Railway at Skovorodino.

The Lena River was long handicapped because its headwaters were not reached by a railway. A line now leaves the Trans-Siberian at Taishet and meets the Lena at Ust Kut. The railway may some day continue eastward to Komsomolsk on the Amur River as part of the proposed B.A.M., or Baikal-Amur Magistral.

The climate is the driest and coldest of any Siberian region yet considered. Precipitation is from 6 to 12 inches, and snowfall amounts to little over a foot. Yearly temperature averages are below freezing, so that a continental ice sheet might develop today if there were enough snowfall. There is no evidence of Pleistocene glaciation except in the mountains, presumably because the area has always been dry. The Lena is frozen at Yakutsk for 210 days.

On account of the low rainfall, grasslands replace the taiga in the lowland plains of the central Lena and Vilyui rivers, with resulting black soils. Cultivation is only moderately successful, but a few hundred thousand acres are sown. Barley and wheat can be raised, but hay and vegetables are the chief crops. Many of the native population live by fishing, gathering furs, and raising reindeer.

Navigation on the Lena began when a steamer was brought from Norway in 1878; there are now dozens of steamships. In order to appreciate the size of this region, it is well to remember that it is a thousand miles from Ust Kut on the railway down river to Yakutsk, and another thousand from there to Tiksi on the Arctic Ocean. Coal is supplied from mines north of Yakutsk, where reserves are very large.

Yakutsk, the one city of importance, serves as the capital for the million square miles of the Yakut Autonomous Soviet Socialist Republic. Founded in 1632, the city has broad muddy streets, plank sidewalks, and one-story log houses, plus a number of brick buildings. The city is poorly located on a low terrace at the inside of a bend on a shallow branch of the Lena. The river, here full of islands and 15 miles wide, is shifting away from the town so that boats must unload four miles away at low water. Floods frequently inundate the city.

Northeastern Mountains

This region continues the system of young mountains that cross Eurasia from the Alps to Kamchatka. The Northeastern Mountains are so inaccessible that the Cherski Range, rising to 9,843 feet, was not discovered until 1926. Kamchatka has the largest group of active volcanoes on the continent, with 127 cones, of which 19 are active. The highest is Mt. Kliuchevskaya, 15,912 feet, which has erupted 19 times in two centuries. In 1907, the volcano Shtiubelia ejected four billion cubic yards of ashes, and some of the dust fell in Europe.

The Northeastern Mountains have long been known as the icebox of

Eurasia. No inhabited place outside Antarctica has observed such bitterly cold winter conditions as this area. Extremely low temperatures are partly related to the winter high pressure over Siberia and also to intense radiation in calm air and local air drainage into enclosed basins. Verkhoyansk has a January average of –57° F. and an absolute minimum of –92.3° F. Observations at Oimyakon show that winters are consistently colder with a January average of –67° F., so that it may come to replace Verkhoyansk as the station with the extreme minimum. The unattractive character of the Oimyakon district is indicated by its population of 3,000 people in an area of 27,000 square miles. In contrast, summer days may rise to 100° F.

In czarist days all of this region was regarded as outside the limits of possible cultivation. Agricultural experiment stations have since shown that some vegetables may be grown in the southern half, including the central valley of Kamchatka. Most of the mainland receives as little precipitation as the Aral-Balkhash Desert, but monsoon winds from the Pacific bring 40 inches to the southeastern part of the Kamchatka Peninsula.

The Okhotsk Sea and the waters around Kamchatka have long been important fishing grounds. Since the catch must be sun dried, the cloudy and foggy weather of the summer presents problems. From 1847 to 1871, American whalers secured whale oil and bone here to the value of $87,500,000; and whales are still caught. Under the Treaty of Portsmouth, which ended the Russo-Japanese War of 1904–1905, Japanese fishermen were given special concessions in this area, and the gradual restriction of these arrangements was the source of much political friction. Salmon, cod, herring, and crab are caught. The chief port on Kamchatka is Petropavlovsk, founded in 1741 and located on one of the world's finest harbors. The port is the most important Soviet harbor on the open Pacific, and had a population of 86,000 in 1959.

The mining of gold on the upper Kolyma started in 1929, and an automobile road leads south to the port of Magadan on the Sea of Okhotsk.

Far East

Southeastern Siberia borders the Pacific and is made up of the southern half of the Khabarovsk Krai, the Amur Oblast, and the Maritime Autonomous Oblast. The heart of the geographic region here considered is the Amur Basin.

The decade prior to the Second World War was marked by a great increase in cultivated land, the beginnings of heavy industry, the growth of cities, and active immigration which brought the population to over two million. With its empty spaces coming into use, the Far East is now nearly self-sufficient in its food and industrial needs.

The Amur is the great river of the east, comparable in size and importance to the three north-flowing Siberian rivers. The chief tributaries on the left bank are the Zeya and Bureya, while on the right the Sungari comes from Manchuria, and the Ussuri forms the eastern Manchurian border. Along the central Amur around Khabarovsk is a broad plain which continues up the Ussuri to Lake Khanka. On the east, the Ussuri lowland is enclosed by the Sikhota Alin Mountains, while on the west are the Long White and Little Khingan mountains.

The Far East has an east coast continental climate which is modified by the Pacific monsoons. Strong dry winter winds blow from the interior, bringing temperatures far below freezing. In summer, relatively warm oceanic air imports moisture, bringing an annual rainfall of 21 inches to Vladivostok. Although Vladivostok lies in the latitude of southern Crimea, its east coast position causes winter temperatures to be 45° colder, resembling those of Halifax.

The flora is of the Manchurian type, with magnificent stands of Korean pine, spruce, fir, and larch, mixed with 10 per cent of deciduous forms such as oak. Meadows cover the drier interior basins.

Few other parts of Siberia east of the Ob have such good agricultural possibilities. Korean immigrant farmers even raise rice north of Vladivostok. Wheat, rye, oats, and barley are the chief grains; sugar beets are grown extensively. Spring planting is delayed, since the ground freezes to ten feet or more under the thin snow cover, and thawing takes place slowly under the cloudy skies of June.

Since the Far East did not formerly raise enough food to supply itself, agricultural colonists from overcrowded parts of Soviet Europe were offered free transportation, credits, and tax exemption. The Jewish colony of Birobidzhan, west of Khabarovsk, is especially interesting in this connection. Jews heretofore had no district that was exclusively their own. This "Soviet Palestine" provides such a national homeland and at the same time strengthens the regional economy.

The Far East contains mineral resources for a growing industry. The Buryea Valley has coal, and low grade iron ore is available from the Little Khingan and lower Amur areas. Lead and zinc have long been secured along the Japan Sea. Coal is also mined near Vladivostok.

Komsomolsk is the magic city of the east. Although founded only in 1932, its population reached 177,000 by 1959. This is the "city of youth," once the lodestone of enthusiastic workers from all over the

Union. Situated on the lower Amur, it has shipyards and the largest steel mills in the Soviet Far East.

Khabarovsk has developed where the Trans-Siberian Railway spans the Amur, and is the political and commercial center of the area.

Vladivostok has a picturesque setting on Peter the Great Bay. The city's trade increased greatly during the First and Second World Wars, and during periods of favorable political relations with Manchuria, but in other years there has been little international commerce. The harbor is kept open through most of the year by icebreakers.

The Far East offers considerable promise. Soils and climate make agriculture relatively attractive. Timber reserves are excellent, minerals are fairly abundant, and transportation is rapidly improving. Many of the people are pioneers, and this "new east" somewhat resembles Canada's "great west." It is probable, however, that Vladivostok will long remain Russia's back door. The Soviet Union is not likely to become a great power in the Pacific.

Vladivostok is the Union's main window on the Pacific, with a picturesque location on Peter the Great Bay. This is a view of Lenin Street. (*Courtesy U.S.S.R. National Committee, I.G.U.*)

Sakhalin and the Kuriles

East of the Soviet mainland lies the elongated island of Sakhalin, once half-owned by Japan but entirely Soviet territory since the Second World War. Prior to 1905, there was a period of Russian control and, still earlier, informal Japanese and Russian claims that date back to the seventeenth century. In 1875, Japan agreed to give up Sakhalin while Russia in turn withdrew from the Kuriles. The Japanese then gave the southern half of the island its old Ainu name of Karafuto.

Sakhalin is cold. Winter lasts six months, and snow covers the island to an average depth of three feet, so that dog sleds are in common use. The summer monsoon is the season of greatest rainfall, but the annual precipitation is only 25 inches. Records of seven meteorological stations show rain or snow every day in the year except for 22 to 53 days. Most ports are icebound for long periods, and the loading of oil tankers in the northern half of the island is impossible for eight months. At some

The island of Sakhalin supplies timber, oil, and coal, and its surrounding waters provide valuable fishing grounds. This is a view of the port of Korsakov. (*Courtesy Soviet Embassy, Washington*)

ports occasional winter steamers tie up at the ice margin offshore and transport goods to the land across the ice.

Two mountain chains on the island limit level land to narrow coastal fragments and a central lowland. Soils are podsolic and of low fertility.

The wealth of Sakhalin lies in its timber, fish, oil, and coal. Agriculture is expanding, but only slowly. Optimistic estimates suggest that there is a modest amount of potentially arable land, but poor soil, short growing seasons, and limited sunshine restrict agricultural possibilities. Chief crops are oats, fodder, potatoes, and peas, in that order.

Fishing is the oldest occupation, and poor villages border many bays. Herring, sea trout, salmon, cod, and crab are the chief catch, in that order. Canned crab meat is an important export to the United States.

Many of those who fish during the summer months work as lumbermen in the winter. Coniferous forests with dense undergrowth cover many of the mountains, interspersed with patches of tundra. Trees are usually small, and forest fires may be serious. Spruce is cut for pulpwood and paper, and there are also fir, larch, birch, elm, and willow. Mine props, railroad ties, and charcoal are important, but pulp is by far the most valuable product. At Shiretori the Japanese built what was reported to be the largest and most modern pulp plant in eastern Asia. The total value of lumbering exceeds that of fishing.

Coal reserves are moderate, and the quality is low. The production is mainly used on the island for railroads and other needs. Considerable oil is secured, chiefly at Okha in the northern half of the island. This is the chief producing area in the eastern Soviet Union.

East of Sakhalin a chain of islands extends northeastward from Japanese Hokkaido to the tip of Soviet Kamchatka. These were known to the Japanese as the Chishima, or thousand islands, but are better known to foreigners by their Russian names of Kuriles, which means "smoke." Actually there are but 32 islands, mostly volcanic. Precipitous cliffs fringe the shores, and there is virtually no agricultural land. Snow falls from mid-September to June, and there is much fog in summer.

The Kuriles are surrounded by valuable fishing grounds which formerly attracted a large number of Japanese boats in summer. Salmon, cod, and crab are important. On the islands are large bears, fox, and sable. Fur seals and sea otter have been protected since the 1911 treaty between Japan, Russia, Great Britain, and the United States.

The Soviet Far East together with Sakhalin and the Kuriles have a maritime environment, quite different from the continental interior. In latitude and potential they somewhat resemble Nova Scotia, Newfoundland, and Labrador.

Chapter IX

INTERNATIONAL RELATIONS

THE LAND of the Soviet Union, under whatever government, is clearly assured of an important future, but that future will be related to unusual environmental situations. The leaders have set as their economic goal: "to overtake and surpass the capitalist world." From the standpoint of geography this scarcely appears possible; if ever achieved it will be because of totalitarian procedures and hard work. Limitations of high latitude, rigorous climate, poor soils, and continentality combine to create unfavorable landscapes which no amount of planning can fully surmount. On the other hand, vast mineral resources and large area are major assets.

The Domestic Base

Two conclusions stand out in any survey of Soviet political geography: this is a rapidly growing country, in a unique continental environment. Each of these has its bearing on national policy, both domestic and foreign.

It will be decades before the Union fully develops its resources of land and minerals; it is likely that its economy will continue to expand for most of the twentieth century. There is still need for thousands

The Soviet airline "Aeroflot" provides regular service to China, North Korea, India, and many centers in Central and Western Europe. These "TU 104" 100-passenger jet planes are at the Vnukovo airport at Moscow. (*Courtesy Soviet Embassy, Washington*)

of miles of new railroads, and for the increase of agricultural production. There are many mines to be developed and scores of factories to be built. These material aspects of pioneering will continue to provide a genuine basis for patriotism. One may assume that it will be the firm policy of the government to press for further internal development, and that domestic progress will take priority ahead of imperialistic goals. Soviet citizens have caught a vision of what their country may become, and they do not want another war to interrupt its progress.

Soviet economic developments during the mid-century period somewhat parallel those in the United States after the Civil War. Spurred by the knowledge that they were living in a rich and vast country, Americans during the nineteenth and early twentieth century devoted much of their energies to carving an empire out of the wilderness, building new railroads, developing new states, creating new cities. A similar upsurge of development is taking place in the U.S.S.R.

The continentality of the U.S.S.R., characterized in geographic terms by climatic extremes and remoteness from the ocean, also serves to isolate the country from stimulating international contacts and outside ideas. Here is a nation which is poorly situated for foreign trade or for international political operations. The Soviets may believe in world-wide communism, and the Kremlin serves as an ideological center, but the Soviet Union provides a poor geographic base from which to dominate the earth; Moscow is oriented internally rather than toward the world outside.

Objectives Abroad

Soviet foreign policy stems from motives so complex that the geographer can do no more than evaluate certain geographic aspects, leaving the political conclusions to others. Three fundamental motives appear in her foreign relations; these are ideologic, economic, and strategic.

It is clear that the Soviet Union desires to spread Marxist-Leninist communism, but many observers in the Western world are uncertain as to how large a factor world-wide revolution may be in present-day Soviet foreign policy. The ideological situation is conflicting, for some statements by Soviet leaders seem to make war inevitable. Inconsistencies thus make it difficult to determine the extent to which Soviet foreign policy turns on aiding world communism. While an examination of Soviet geography may not reveal Soviet political motives, it does serve to substantiate Stalin's belief that the U.S.S.R. has the human and material resources to create a socialist state, independently of world revolution.

On the other hand, the study of Soviet geography provides a considerable understanding of the economic motives underlying Soviet foreign policy. No country is so nearly self-sufficient as the U.S.S.R. The Union would like to buy a long list of raw materials and specialized products from abroad, but the need is not imperative. The import situation is totally different from that in Britain, or even in the United States. America cannot operate its present economy without large imports; it needs tin, asbestos, manganese, chromium, and a host of other things; not so in the Soviet Union.

While domestic production in the U.S.S.R. has expanded greatly, demand has so far fully kept pace. There is thus little surplus production which must be disposed of abroad in order to keep the domestic economy moving. For the most part, the economic advantage of export is limited; indeed, export may even delay meeting domestic goals. This is certainly the case with almost all manufactured goods; it is normally true of grain, but is not the case with manganese, gold, oil, or a few other surplus materials. The situation may change within a decade, since the capacity for primary production is becoming so large that supplies may surpass internal needs.

The Soviet Union would doubtless like to trade, and may be expected to do so under normal conditions, but it is not an essential factor in economic policy. It should be remembered, too, that many of the producing and consuming centers are far from tidewater, so that international commerce must bear a heavy freight charge for rail or river shipment in addition to ocean transport.

Resources in bordering countries which might prove politically as well as economically attractive to the Soviet Union include uranium from Czechoslovakia, chromium from Turkey, tin and tungsten from China, and oil from Iran. Special mineral needs are illustrated by the Union's annexation of northern Finland with its nickel mine.

Foreign trade agreements frequently represent political gestures rather than economic need, as the shipment of wheat to France or to India, or the delivery of machinery to Cuba. In other words, economic factors alone are not of compelling importance in the framing of foreign policy.

Has the addition of bordering countries such as Poland, Rumania, or China proved to be of economic advantage to the U.S.S.R.? All of these nations once depended upon large imports from the West, both for raw materials and for technical items, which were largely eliminated when the areas came under Soviet influence. In order to maintain the economy of such areas, the Soviet Union had to supply their needs.

Soviet industrial capacity now makes it possible for the Union to export steel products of many kinds. This tube rolling mill is in Azerbaidzhan. (*Courtesy Soviet Embassy, Washington*)

Since the Union had little to spare, especially in earlier decades, the effort undoubtedly put a drain on the Soviet economy, and the returning imports, if any, were of limited importance.

It is especially doubtful whether China has much to offer the U.S.S.R. in return for the very large investment of capital goods which will be needed if China is to develop rapidly. That country does have tin, antimony, and tungsten to spare, but the necessity of repaying Soviet imports with Chinese agricultural products sent to Siberia represents an export which China can ill afford. China may long remain an economic liability, for it is uncertain how China could repay large loans.

If ideologic and economic considerations are the first two items in Soviet foreign policy, strategic matters may be the third. The need for security, a major concern for every nation, is felt especially by the

Soviet peoples, who believe that they live in a hostile world, one which is about to attack them. Their apprehensions may be largely the result of their own propaganda, or may be traced to a number of other factors including Western distrust of Soviet aims. Whatever their origins, Soviet apprehensions are very real. Twice in the twentieth century, and many times before, the country has been invaded, and the Soviet Union is determined that if war comes again it will not be fought on its own soil. A major concern of the Union has thus been to surround itself with a cushion of buffer states.

With minor exceptions, the entire Soviet frontier from Finland to Korea is insulated by buffer states. The one gap is next to Turkey, Iran, and Afghanistan. Here is where the non-communist world impinges directly on Soviet territory. It would be consistent with Kremlin policy to attempt to bring these countries inside the Iron Curtain. One may thus anticipate Soviet pressures in Southwestern Asia. If the Soviet Union could obtain possession of Turkey, Iran, and Afghanistan, and if it could dominate the area between Istanbul and the Persian Gulf, it would complete its corridor of satellite states and secure a position from which it could easily inflict serious economic pressures upon the rest of the world. The Suez Canal and the air routes which pass east and west through Cairo and Beirut are the principle avenues which link Europe and South Asia. If they were blocked, travel might have to go around Africa. And if the Free World were deprived of the petroleum of the Persian Gulf, the West would be severely affected.

Most of the Soviet boundary has excellent natural defenses: frozen seas, wide deserts, high mountains, and uninhabited areas. The only easy approach is from the west, and it is here that security in depth is most needed in order to protect the thick end of the agricultural and population triangle. Territorial security thus appears to be a major consideration in Soviet foreign policy today, with some prospect of further expansion in the form of satellite states.

It is also true that the history of old Russia was one of expansion. This growth was motivated by a desire for political conquest, for economic advantage, and for an outlet to the sea. Starting from centers around Kiev and Moscow, the country expanded in all directions. The quest for seaports may be seen in the acquisition and development of Leningrad, Riga, Odessa, and Vladivostok. One economic motive for the advance into Siberia was the search for salt and for furs.

The quite natural ambition of the Russian Bear to reach additional warm-water ports conflicts with geographic realities. There is no possible gateway to the open ocean which would be accessible to the

Students from many communist countries attend the University of Moscow, whose main building appears in the background. These international students come from Bulgaria, Czechoslovakia, Romania, China, Albania, and Germany. (*Tass*)

center of Soviet population. Even a full command of the Baltic would not bring secure contact with the high seas. Murmansk is open, but off center, and during the Second World War the Germans demonstrated its vulnerability. An advance to the Persian Gulf would provide warm water, but the value of a seaport there would be only marginal. Vladivostok is remote, and icebound for part of the year. Port Arthur and Dairen are open the year around, but are equally distant.

Earlier expansion to the east and south was into areas that were unpopulated or were occupied by people with cultures of limited dimensions; any farther advance now involves difficult problems of assimilation. The Russian people may have to be satisfied with their present living room.

Insofar as communist ideology, economic need, and strategic security are considerations in Soviet foreign relations, it would appear that the last is paramount. This is not just a desire for military protection, but a determination to insure the continuation of internal progress under the program of socialist planning.

Location and Security

Location has long been recognized as one of the key items in national strength, but the value of different situations has changed with time. Through sea power Rome once controlled the Mediterranean, and Britain developed a world-wide empire. The Mongols formerly ruled Eurasia with cavalry, and both Napoleon and Hitler endeavored to build great land powers. Does Russia's intra-continental position give her a secure base for world conquest, or does maritime Europe still hold the advantage through its greater accessibility to the rest of the world?

At the time of the First World War, the British political geographer, Halford J. Mackinder, wrote a small volume entitled "Democratic Ideals and Reality" in which he weighed the course of history in terms of land power versus sea power. Mackinder contended that maritime powers always win in the long run, for they can draw on the entire world for aid. Land powers may occupy a secure castle, almost impossible to attack, but eventually they can be starved out. In modern terms, here is the contest between Britain and Germany, for in both World Wars sea power won.

But as Mackinder surveyed the world, there seemed to be one impregnable castle which no amount of ocean-based attack could subdue. This was Inner Asia, which he termed the Pivot of History, or the Heartland. This secure fortress, the Heartland, is surrounded on the south by the towering Himalaya, on the east by the empty Gobi Desert, and on the north by the frozen Arctic, all of them thought to be uncrossable by an invading army. Only on the west was the castle vulnerable since no physical barrier separates it from Eastern Europe.

Since the Eurasian-African continents, or the World Island, contain two-thirds of the world's land and six-sevenths of its population, Mackinder developed the following sequence:

> Who rules East Europe, commands the Heartland;
> Who rules the Heartland, commands the World Island;
> Who rules the World Island, commands the World.

Writing in 1943, Mackinder found his concept "more valid and useful today than it was twenty or forty years ago" and added that "if the

Soviet Union emerges from the war as conqueror of Germany, she must rank as the greatest land power on the globe. Moreover, she will be the power in the strategically strongest defensive position." *

The extent of the Heartland has been variously defined, and the location of its European gateway ranges from the Urals to a line connecting the Baltic and the Adriatic. It is thus only roughly coextensive with the Soviet Union. Conditions within the area differ widely, and the most highly developed portions are in the West where they are especially vulnerable to invasion, rather than deep within Inner Asia.

Surrounding the Heartland is a crescentic area which Nicholas Spykman, the American political scientist, has called the Rimland. This crescent swings around Eurasia from Britain through India to Japan, and is much more densely populated and accessible to world ideas than the central Pivot Area. Spykman has challenged Mackinder's concept, and has proposed a formula which reads:

> Who controls the Rimland rules Eurasia,
> Who rules Eurasia controls the destinies of the world.

Spykman's ideas reflect the importance of sea power and of international accessibility, and give little weight to the invulnerability of a Heartland. With the expansion of Soviet communism to China, Southeast Asia, and Eastern Germany, the Heartland and Rimland have become partly joined, and the Communist World is indeed a power area.

Despite the superficial attractiveness of Mackinder's concepts, they need to be reinterpreted in terms of the air age. Mountains, deserts, and oceans are no longer barriers, and conquest does not rest on land armies alone. Furthermore, it is not enough that a fortress have impregnable walls; it must have people and supplies. As has been emphasized in this volume, much of the Soviet Union, especially Siberia and Middle Asia, is low in agricultural productivity and hence in population potential. While the mineral wealth is impressive, the problems of transport and trade are difficult.

Progress comes through stimulating contacts, not by withdrawal into a castle, no matter how secure. Endurance in war is seldom greater than economic health in peace. Security through an isolated location appears less dependable than security through intrinsic strength and world-wide allies. The first lesson of geography is interdependence; trade and cultural relations are inescapable.

* Mackinder, Halford J., "The Round World and the Winning of the Peace," *Foreign Affairs*, XXI, p. 601 (1943).

China and the Soviet Union

The Soviet Union and the Mongolian People's Republic border China for over 6,000 miles. No other countries on earth have so long a frontier, nor one which is so sparsely populated. Much of the border lies amid deserts and mountains. The only area where there is a considerable population near the frontier is next to eastern Manchuria; elsewhere the population density on either side of the boundary is less than one person per square mile. Except in the Soviet Far East, there is not a single city of 100,000 people within 100 miles of either side of the border. The situation is not essentially altered by regarding Outer Mongolia as oriented to the north or south. The vast areas between China and the Union are devoid of economic importance.

Only three railways cross the 6,000 miles of frontier; the Trans-

Rugged mountains encircle the U.S.S.R. on the south and east, and thus restrict international trade, as well as moisture-bearing winds. This caravan is in the snow-crowned Pamirs. (*Tass*)

Siberian Railway where it traverses Manchuria, the Trans-Mongolian Railway which provides a short cut from Lake Baikal to Peking, and the new Trans-Chinese Railway which crosses Sinkiang to meet the Turkestan-Siberian line near Lake Balkhash. None of these provides daily passenger service, and the maximum tonnage of freight which might move overland from the Soviet Union into China is of modest proportions.

Not more than a dozen automobile roads cross the border, none of them paved and all long and rough, suitable only for trucks and jeeps. Elsewhere are a few caravan routes or cart roads. All of these involve hundreds of miles through mountains or across arid wastes, and it is unlikely that the potential traffic will justify modernization.

The two countries share the middle part of the Amur River and its tributary the Ussuri, but the only streams which cross the border are the Irtysh and Ili, both in the far west of China.

Air services connect Moscow and Peking via Irkutsk and Mongolia

Murmansk is the Union's only fully ice-free port, but it lies so far off-center that its peacetime use is limited. This steamer, the *Kazakhstan*, is used on the Northern Sea Route during the brief summer navigation season. (*Sovfoto*)

with service through Harbin as well, and an airline links Alma Ata with Tihwa, but distances are so great that only valuable freight justifies the expense of transportation.

The problem of normal international trade between the two nations is primarily a matter of distance and costs. The center of industrial production in the Soviet Union lies near the Volga; in China the center of consumption lies along the Yangtze. These are 4,000 miles apart by airline distance, and nearly 6,000 miles by rail. The Manchuria provinces can barter local wheat for machinery made in the Soviet Far East, and Sinkiang may secure supplies from Soviet Middle Asia, but the major items in any large-scale trade must move thousands of miles.

If the Union of Soviet Socialist Republics and the People's Republic of China should ever develop extensive commerce, it will be cheaper for it to move by sea around the periphery of Asia. Shipping costs by boat from Leningrad or Odessa via Suez and Singapore to Shanghai are much less than overland by rail. Arctic routes are considerably shorter, but are available for only two or three months each year. The mere fact that China and Russia are close neighbors does not imply easy intercourse.

During the nineteenth century and the first half of the twentieth, China had much more contact with Europe and North America than with Russia. Along the China coast are two dozen modern seaports. The combined freight capacity of these ocean gateways may well be a thousand times that of the overland connections. Modern China faces the Pacific, not interior Eurasia.

This was not always so. During much of her early history, China was self-sufficient and foreign trade was negligible. Such external contacts as she had were largely landward. Thus the so-called Jade Gate at the western end of the Great Wall was the avenue for Marco Polo, for Chinese pilgrims who went to India in quest of Buddhism, and for early caravans which carried silk and porcelain to Europe. Ancient China faced landward, and the Pacific was her back door. Modern China has turned about face and looks east, so that the port cities of Dairen, Tientsin, Shanghai, and Canton are her front doors. Any reversal toward the interior, including Soviet connections, would be economically illogical.

The Soviet Union primarily faces westward, as shown in the pattern of the agricultural triangle. On the other hand, the country has the longest Pacific coastline of any nation bordering that ocean. Unfortunately, Russia's coast is also the most useless, for conditions resemble Labrador rather than British Columbia. The Soviet Union clearly desires to strengthen its position along the Pacific, but this will remain the Union's back door because of severe geographic restrictions.

Political and economic interests provide a strategic background for Soviet interests in China. These include access to ice-free ports, and an ideological springboard for communism in South Asia. Russia will not willingly accept a hostile neighbor, and one reason for her large-scale interference in China following the Second World War may have been to prevent China from becoming an American base. It may be doubted whether Russia's heavy investments in China will ever pay off in economic terms, but the strategic and ideological values are great.

Russian relations with China are of long standing. Russia was China's last important customer for tea, which was the traditional item of trade,

The Moscow Stadium seats 100,000 people and is a reminder of the increasing role of the Soviet people in international sports. (*Courtesy Soviet Embassy, Washington*)

with regular caravans moving across Mongolia. Political relations have not always been friendly between the two countries. China once controlled large parts of Siberia, including the present Maritime Province, the area on both sides of Lake Baikal now known as Buriat Mongolia, and large sections of Soviet Middle Asia almost to the Caspian Sea. Chinese writers, both Nationalist and Communist, list these areas as "stolen by czarist Russia"; they total 816,000 square miles. China's legal claim to these lost territories may be vague, but here is a possible source of future friction.

The two countries are quite different. China's population is three times that of Russia's, but her area is only two-fifths as large. China's terrain and climate are varied, but some of the soil is superior to any in the Union. China has only 450,000 square miles of crop land, with little possibility of increase, as compared with 600,000 square miles in the Soviet Union. An insufficient food supply for its large population is one of China's basic problems.

Another important difference lies in mineral wealth and economic potential. China has great deposits of coal, but her reserves of petroleum and several metals appear limited. There is natural wealth enough to start significant industrialization but apparently not enough to enable China to match Soviet achievements.

The United States Joint Congressional Committee on Atomic Energy has evaluated Chinese fuel resources as compared with those of Russia, as follows:

China possesses the only significant reserves of primary energy known to exist in the Asiatic portion of the Sino-Soviet Area. Based on fragmentary data which undoubtedly have high margins of error, it is estimated that China has primary energy reserves equal to about 1.4 trillion tons of standard fuel. This would indicate that China's primary fuel reserves are equal to about 20 per cent of those of the U.S.S.R.

"As in other parts of the Sino-Soviet Area, the largest share (about 98%) of the energy reserve is composed of coal. Second to coal are oil shale reserves of more than 20 billion tons of standard fuel. Although relatively unimportant in the picture of total reserves, the hydroelectric potential of China, like that of the U.S.S.R. probably will play a significant role in the economic development of China.

"To date there is little reliable evidence upon which to base an estimate of China's natural crude oil reserves. Present estimates place

proved reserves of natural crude oil at 30 million tons and possible
reserves at 1.3 billion tons. In addition reserves of oil shale could
yield as much as 15 billion tons of oil.*

The balance between population and resources in the United States
is roughly comparable to that in the Soviet Union, thus the Soviets may
hope to emulate America. However, China's balance is far different.
In terms of China's vast population and limited arable land, and notwithstanding its mineral assets, the prospects are for one of the lowest
per capita incomes of any great nation. The food supply promises to
be especially precarious.

Chinese communism looks to Karl Marx and to Lenin, and is grateful
for Soviet economic aid, but China cannot be regarded as a Russian
satellite. The situation is quite different from that of the much smaller
European allies. China has profited by following the Soviet line, but
Peking will deviate from Moscow when it becomes in China's interest
to do so.

Chinese culture is so old and rich, her area is so vast and diverse,
and her population is so large and capable that her integrity seems
assured. China will retain direction of its own affairs, even though it
continues as a communist state. It is well to recall that following its
first acceptance of Soviet aid in 1927, China turned out the Soviet
advisers as soon as current objectives had been achieved.

It is interesting to speculate as to whether China, which has had
imperialistic ventures in the past, will again develop territorial objectives when it becomes modernized, and if so, what these objectives
will be. The China of tomorrow will need food and raw materials for
industry. The parts of Siberia which are accessible to China offer
little in the way of agricultural land. Only by moving thousands of
miles overland into western Siberia would the Chinese succeed in lo-
cating large supplies of food. Siberia has coal and some iron, which
China does not need, but has little near-by oil which China lacks. Thus,
Siberia offers little to interest China, which may instead look southward
to the peninsulas and islands of Southeast Asia where the attractions are
greater and the probable resistance less.

Over the centuries, China has been the leading power in East Asia,

* U.S. Congress, Joint Congressional Committee on Atomic Energy, *Background
Material for the Review of International Atomic Policies and Programs of the
United States*, IV, p. 1646. Washington: Government Printing Office (Oct. 1960).

and within a few decades this may again be the case. Soviet assistance has been of major value, but China is now able to advance on the basis of her own skills and resources. The strategic association has been mutually advantageous, and may continue, but in economic terms China has the ability to carry on alone should nationalism so dictate.

Chapter X

SOVIET POTENTIALS

MANY FACTORS bear upon Soviet potentials, some within the scope of geography, others matters of ideology or government. To fully weigh the prospects for the Union of Soviet Socialist Republics requires far more than a single volume or the contribution of a single discipline.

A Geographic Check List

The following check list includes some of the specific aspects of geography which bear on the internal development and international relations of the U.S.S.R. None of the items are deterministic, but they do represent background situations. In the physical field the components of power analysis involve the ten items of location, size and shape, landforms, climate, natural vegetation, soils, minerals, sources of energy, inland waters, and maritime relations. On the human side there are ten other components, including the numbers and distribution of people, social development, food supply, industry, government, communications and accessibility, international trade, boundaries, neighboring countries, and time. The following paragraphs provide a quick assessment of Soviet political prospects in terms of each item.

Location is the primary fact in any national analysis. The Soviet Union is a high-latitude country, much of it deep within the largest

The Exhibition of Economic Achievement in Moscow provides a survey of Soviet development. The main building is surrounded by pavilions from each of the 15 republics; that of the Kazakh S.S.R. is shown at the right. (*Courtesy Sovinform-bureau, Moscow*)

continent. No other country has so much land in arctic regions, or is so remote from the oceans. While the Union appears to occupy a central position in Eurasia, in effective terms it is off-center for both Europe and Asia. This land-locked interior position is a constant, but its significance changes with developments in transportation and strategy. Thus in time of war an interior location may enable a nation to shift troops easily from one front to another. While the Union borders many nations, the eastern and southern contacts are across mountains and deserts, and her immediate neighbors on the west are of junior stature.

Size and shape have obvious importance. Some nations are so small that they lack a desirable variety of environments or resources, or cannot defend their territory against aggressive neighbors. One reason why Russia survived the invasions of Napoleon, the Kaiser, and Hitler is that the country had room into which she might retreat, gradually exchanging space for time. Too large a size may present difficulties of unity and coherence, so that Soviet administration of eight and a half

Climate is an ever present factor in Soviet potentials; millions of square miles are too cold or too dry for normal settlement. This is a view on the Samm Collective Farm near Murmansk where tractors compete with reindeer. (*Photo by V. Shustov*)

million square miles has been a major problem. Irregular shape presents obvious political difficulties, not always appreciated until seen in terms of the effective territory. Thus the U.S.S.R. appears compact until one examines the ribbon character of settlement in Siberia.

Soviet landforms are diverse, with great rolling plains in the west and center, bordered by high mountains in the south and east. The former provide a suitable terrain for agriculture and offer few obstacles to transportation, while the latter serves to defend and isolate the Union from its neighbors. Nearly half of the Union's vast area is too mountainous or too hilly to provide a good habitat for a dense population, but on the whole the political aspects of Russia's terrain are favorable for internal development, except for invasion dangers on the west.

Climate is one of Russia's great handicaps, for winters are so long and severe that little outdoor activity is possible. On the other hand, continentality brings wide seasonal contrasts so that the short summers may have hot days with long hours of daylight. The precipitation is generally low, no more than 20 inches in most cultivated areas or half that of the eastern United States. The short growing season and uncertain rainfall place serious limitations on the food supply. Millions of square miles are too cold or too dry for normal agriculture, and will always have a sparse population. Other millions are underlain by permanently frozen ground. On the other hand, the wide range in latitude provides for a considerable variation in temperatures and crops. The core area of relatively favorable climate covers a million square miles, of which only 600,000 square miles are actually cultivated.

Natural vegetation is both a resource and an indicator of agricultural possibilities. The Soviet Union contains the world's largest forest, but half of it has doubtful commercial value. Hardwoods are in short supply in most of the country. To understand the natural cover of vegetation is to evaluate the climate, terrain, soil, and land use potential.

While the Union has large areas of chernozem soils, rich but marginally dry, the bulk of the country is underlain by podsol soils of modest fertility. Elsewhere there are unproductive tundra or desert soils, or wide swamp lands. The Union's good soils are already in full use, and the chief areas of new cultivation involve soils which are moderately fertile but dangerously dry. In purely physical terms, Soviet soils are adequate to feed her people but offer no great promise for the future. The soils of the Ukraine have twice been a temptation for German conquest.

Mineral wealth appears to be one of the major keys to political power in the twentieth century, and in this respect the Union of Soviet Socialist Republics is outstanding. Iron, aluminum, copper, manganese, and a long list of resources are present in abundance. In several instances the quality or location is poor, but the total reserves of metals and the non-metals are impressive. The Union appears to lead the world in several commodities, and is more nearly self-sufficient in its mineral wealth than any other nation.

Energy is as important as are minerals, and the U.S.S.R. is abundantly supplied with coal, oil, gas, and hydroelectricity. Less is known about reserves of fissionable minerals, but they appear adequate. Insofar as fossil fuels and water power are keys to economic strength, and this in turn to political importance, the Union ranks very high.

Inland waterways, including rivers, canals, and lakes, have always presented a problem because they are blocked by ice for many months, and because most rivers fail to reach the open ocean. Much attention has been given to an integrated waterway system, especially that which links the Volga with the Baltic and Black Seas. Thus, small vessels may move from the Arctic along interior waterways to the Mediterranean. Fortunately, the Union controls the mouths of all of its rivers, and only one major frontier follows a navigable river, namely the Amur next to China.

The Union's maritime contacts are limited by the frozen Arctic and by constricted outlets to the open Atlantic and Pacific. While the country faces three oceans, access to the high seas is nowhere easy. Seaports should provide one of the main contacts between nations, but conditions are unfavorable around most of the Union. Only Murmansk is ice-free, and it is far off center. Vladivostok can usually be kept open, but it leads to the enclosed Sea of Japan. Other Pacific ports are backed by high mountains. Access to the Black Sea is of limited wartime value without control of the Bosporus, the Aegean Islands, and Gibraltar, and the Baltic Seas are controlled by the waters around Denmark. Nowhere does the Russian Bear find warm water.

These ten physical situations are relatively constant; what man does with them is quite another matter. Minerals are of little practical value until above ground, seas may be frozen but can be penetrated by ice breakers, deserts can be irrigated, and planes can fly over mountains. The following ten cultural components of political geography may thus outweigh the purely physical factors. Dynamic ideas can make a weak nation powerful, at least for a time. Communism is clearly more explosive than czarism as a political philosophy.

Soviet rivers are being linked by canals to form an integrated system of inland waterways. Here is the Volga at the city of Gorki. (*Photo by Y. Berliner*)

People are the most important of all the elements in Soviet geography. In numbers they rank third after China and India. When plotted on a map, however, it is clear that only a small part of the national territory is occupied. Some regions are congested, while others are uninhabited. Political power must be considered in terms of where people live. For some of the country, the problem is one of under-development, but the rapid growth of population may soon bring an end to effective pioneer expansion. Within the Union are many non-Slavic races, most of which are given separate political status. Few Soviet internal or external boundaries mark distinct ethnic divisions; problems thus arise with people who live on both sides of an international border, as in the case of Armenians who also live in Iran, or the Karelians who spread into Finland.

Social development is less easy to measure, but the emphasis placed by the Soviet Union on education and especially on technology has become dramatically evident in recent years. What was a backward country in the nineteenth century is becoming a modern society, and this is true even in remote areas. One facet of culture concerns ideals

The Soviets have continued the high tradition of the theatre developed in czarist days; every major city has its opera house. This is a view of Theatre Square in Tashkent, capital of the Uzbek Republic. (*Photo by Dm. Chernov*)

and motives, and here it must be recognized that many citizens in the Soviet Union have been captured by a dynamic political and economic idea—the desire to develop the world's first socialist state. Communism thus has geographic importance.

Food represents a major problem in Soviet geography. Crop yields fluctuate, and there is still occasional danger of local famine, but in general people are adequately fed. As population grows, so must the food supply, and this presents some difficulties. There is little prospect of an export surplus; in fact, imports from China and the European satellites include supplies of grain. In the long run, the U.S.S.R. must solve its food problem at home.

Soviet industry has blossomed with spectacular success under the successive economic plans. The Union now leads all Europe in total industrial output and is surpassed only by the United States. Per capita production is another matter. So far, this industrial capacity has been directed largely to producer goods, but when the official policy gives attention to consumer items the progress could be rapid. Soviet capabilities in steel and primary production are very impressive. It would be entirely possible for Russia to develop a large export trade in manufactured products, and if costs were disregarded such trade might disrupt international commerce.

The form of a nation's government may be a non-geographic item, but it assumes geographic meaning when the area under the control of a government is plotted on a map. In the case of the U.S.S.R. this must include the various categories of satellite and related states, both adjoining and distant. Moscow is both the capital of the U.S.S.R. and of world communism. The world would rest easier if it could be certain whether the Kremlin's foreign policy is motivated by fear of invasion or plan for conquest; is the prime objective internal development and peaceful coexistence or does it involve imperial goals?

Communication facilities and internal accessibility reflect the coherence of a nation. The free circulation of people, goods, and ideas is essential to a unified state, especially to one as large as Russia. The U.S.S.R. has a closely spaced railway net west of the Urals but large areas in the east are hundreds of miles from a railway. Highways are poor everywhere except near the largest cities. In a country of such great distances, air service is obviously valuable, and in this respect the Union has made notable progress.

International trade plays an increasing role in Soviet economy, at times largely for political reasons, but few imports represent absolute essentials. Among Soviet deficiencies are tropical items such as rubber, coffee, vegetable oils, and fibres; among the surplus commodities are petroleum, manganese, and gold. It was probably a strain on the internal economy to help other communist states during the 1950's, and in overall balance the satellites may have been more of an economic liability than an asset; their strategic value is quite another matter. As industry develops in the Soviet Union, the country might become a substantial exporter; here again, limited access to the high seas is a handicap.

Boundary problems have characterized Russia since the early days. Every century and almost every decade have seen territorial changes. In places the frontiers have reached what might be termed natural limits, as along the Siberian mountains or the swamps adjoining Poland. Elsewhere the political border has moved beyond the physical frontier, as in the Caucasus.

The Second World War involved boundary readjustments next to Finland, the reacquisition of Estonia, Latvia, and Lithuania, the conquest of eastern Prussia and a third of Poland, the addition of Ruthenia from Hungary and Northern Bucovina from Romania, along with the annexation of southern Sakhalin and the Kurile Islands from Japan. Tanna Tuva and the Kushka area of Afghanistan were annexed in 1946. Mongolia has long been a Soviet satellite, though Chinese influence is returning. During the 1940's, the Union added 262,957 square miles with a population of 23,000,000, in addition to her control over satel-

Within a few decades, Soviet industry has grown from that of a backward state to a modern nation, although the development has been uneven. This factory near Gorki assembles the Volga automobile. (*Photographer unknown*)

lite states. Disputed areas in Turkey and Iran have repeatedly been the subject of Soviet pressures.

The prospects for boundary stability may be measured by looking across the frontiers to discover whether there are assets which the Soviet Union especially needs. The U.S.S.R. has few urgent resource requirements, but oil in northern Iran and around the Persian Gulf might represent an attraction. Freer access to the Atlantic led the Union to hold Denmark's Bornholm Island for several years following the Second World War. Afghanistan is attractive because it provides an avenue to Pakistan and India. Manchuria offers rich soil and direct access to the Yellow Sea. Soviet acquisition of the Kurile Islands was undoubtedly designed to open unrestricted contact with the Pacific.

A nation's neighbors are clearly of geographic importance, whether they be friend or foe. Few parts of the Soviet boundary can be regarded as fully stable, and none of its neighbors are dependably friendly. Only next to Finland, Turkey, Iran, and Afghanistan does the Union directly confront the "Free World"; as long as security is a major factor in Soviet policy these non-satellite border lands will be under pressure.

Time changes many political situations. Lithuania once ruled lands to the Black Sea, but this was so long ago that no valid claim remains. Although China and the Soviet Union are in alliance, boundary problems remain. Soviet interests in the Bosporus are merely quiescent.

In the air age deserts and oceans disappear as obstacles, and location must be revalued. Many of the foregoing paragraphs have been based on conventional relations by land and sea. The Arctic has been a barrier between Asia and North America; will it in time become an aerial avenue? Can India and the Soviet Union look forward to close relations as planes fly across the Himalaya?

Certain basic geographic factors will continue to influence Russian policy. These include the desire for internal resource development, additional food supply, freer access to the high seas, enlarged foreign trade, and the achievement of security. While Soviet potentials are impressive, the environmental limitations are also important. Irrespective of her form of government, it does not seem likely that the land of the Soviets can overtake Western Europe or North America in overall material strength and per capita welfare.

STATISTICAL TABLES

POLITICAL STRUCTURE

Republic	Square Kilometers‡	Square Miles†	Republics, Oblasts, Krays, and Okrugs‡	Urban Type Settlements‡
Russian S.F.S.R.	17,075,400	6,593,391	88	1,296
Ukrainian S.S.R.	601,000	232,046	26	497
Byelorussian S.S.R.	207,600	80,154	7	96
Estonian S.S.R.	45,100	17,413	0	28
Latvian S.S.R.	63,700	24,595	0	27
Lithuanian S.S.R.	65,200	25,174	0	9
Moldavian S.S.R.	33,700	13,012	0	18
Azerbaidzhan S.S.R.	86,600	33,436	2	91
Georgian S.S.R.	69,700	26,911	3	32
Armenian S.S.R.	29,200	11,506	0	21
Kazakh S.S.R.	2,756,000	1,064,082	16	136
Turkmen S.S.R.	488,000	188,417	4	60
Uzbek S.S.R.	409,400	158,069	10	51
Kirgiz S.S.R.	195,500	76,641	5	31
Tadzhik S.S.R.	142,500	55,019	2	30
U.S.S.R.	22,402,200	8,650,069*	163	2,423

* Including the territorial area of the

White Sea	34,749
Sea of Azov	15,444

† Britannica Book of the Year, 1961

‡ Central Statistical Administration, Council of Ministers, U.S.S.R., *The National Economy of the U.S.S.R.*, Moscow: Statistical Publishing House (1956).

Urban and Rural Population

Republic	1939* Total	1959† Urban	1959† Rural	1959† Total
Russian S.F.S.R.	108,379,000	61,477,000	56,017,000	117,494,000
Ukrainian S.S.R.	40,469,000	19,130,000	22,763,000	41,893,000
Byelorussian S.S.R.	8,910,000	2,475,000	5,585,000	8,060,000
Uzbek S.S.R.	6,336,000	2,720,000	5,393,000	8,113,000
Kazakh S.S.R.	6,094,000	4,069,000	5,232,000	9,301,000
Georgian S.S.R.	3,540,000	1,696,000	2,353,000	4,049,000
Azerbaidzhan S.S.R.	3,205,000	1,765,000	1,935,000	3,700,000
Lithuanian S.S.R.	2,880,000	1,045,000	1,668,000	2,713,000
Moldavian S.S.R.	2,452,000	639,000	2,241,000	2,880,000
Latvian S.S.R.	1,885,000	1,173,000	921,000	2,094,000
Kirgiz S.S.R.	1,458,000	692,000	1,371,000	2,063,000
Tadzhik S.S.R.	1,484,000	645,000	1,337,000	1,982,000
Armenian S.S.R.	1,282,000	884,000	884,000	1,768,000
Turkmenian S.S.R.	1,252,000	698,000	822,000	1,520,000
Estonian S.S.R.	1,052,000	674,000	522,000	1,196,000
Union of Soviet Socialist Republics	170,191,000	99,777,695	108,848,955	208,826,650

* Data for 1939 includes estimates for territories incorporated along western boundaries, so that 1939 and 1959 figures apply to same areas.
† *Pravda*, May 10, 1959.

Soviet Nationalities*

Nationality	Census 1959	Research Workers 1955
Russians	114,588,000	114,285
Ukrainians	36,981,000	21,762
Byelorussians	7,829,000	4,077
Uzbeks	6,004,000	1,577
Tatars	4,969,000	2,142
Kazakhs	3,581,000	1,172
Azerbaidzhans	2,929,000	2,779
Armenians	2,787,000	5,089
Georgians	2,650,000	5,271
Lithuanians	2,326,000	1,741
Jews	2,268,000	24,620
Moldavians	2,214,000	305
Germans	1,619,000	—
Chuvashes	1,470,000	398
Latvians	1,400,000	1,764
Tadzhiks	1,397,000	359
Poles	1,380,000	—

continued

Mordvins	1,285,000	212
Turkmens	1,004,000	232
Bashkirs	983,000	219
Kirgiz	974,000	289
Estonians	969,000	1,568
Dagestan people	945,000	231
Udmurts	623,000	90
Mari	504,000	71

* *Pravda*, Feb. 4, 1960

Urban Populations by Geographic Regions
(all cities over 200,000)

Region and City	1959 Census	Republic
SOVIET EUROPE		
Ukrainia		
Kiev	1,102,000	Ukrainian
Kharkov	930,000	Ukrainian
Donets	701,000	Ukrainian
Odessa	667,000	Ukrainian
Dnepropetrovsk	658,000	Ukrainian
Rostov-on-Don	597,000	Ukrainian
Zaporozhe	435,000	Ukrainian
Lvov	410,000	Ukrainian
Krivoi Rog	386,000	Ukrainian
Makeevka	358,000	Ukrainian
Gorlovka	293,000	Ukrainian
Zhdanov	284,000	Ukrainian
Lugansk	274,000	Ukrainian
Nikolaev	224,000	Ukrainian
Kursk	203,000	Ukrainian
Taganrog	201,000	Ukrainian
Dneprodzerzhinsk	194,000	Ukrainian
Byelorussia		
Minsk	509,000	Byelorussian
Baltic States		
Riga	605,000	Latvian
Tallin	280,000	Estonian
Vilnius	235,000	Lithuanian
Kaliningrad	202,000	Russian
Metropolitan Leningrad		
Leningrad	3,300,000	Russian
Kola-Karelia		
Murmansk	226,000	Russian
Dvina-Pechora Taiga		
Arkhangelsk	256,000	Russian

continued

Central Agricultural Region		
Gorki	942,000	Russian
Kazan	643,000	Russian
Yaroslavl	406,000	Russian
Tula	345,000	Russian
Ivanovo	332,000	Russian
Izhevsk	283,000	Russian
Kalinin	261,000	Russian
Kirov	252,000	Russian
Ulyanovsk	205,000	Russian
Metropolitan Moscow		
Moscow	5,032,000	Russian
Southern Agricultural Region		
Kuibyshev	806,000	Russian
Volgagrad	591,000	Russian
Saratov	581,000	Russian
Voronezh	454,000	Russian
Penza	254,000	Russian
Chkalov	260,000	Russian
Urals		
Sverdlovsk	777,000	Russian
Chelyabinsk	688,000	Russian
Perm	628,000	Russian
Ufa	546,000	Russian
Nizhni Tagil	338,000	Russian
Magnitogorsk	311,000	Russian
MIDDLE ASIA		
Caucasia		
Baku	968,000	Azerbaidzhan
Tbilisi	694,000	Georgian
Yerevan	509,000	Armenian
Krasnodar	312,000	Russian
Caspian Desert		
Astrakhan	294,000	Russian
Pamir Highlands		
Dushanbe	224,000	Tadzhik
Frunze	217,000	Kirgiz
Turan Oases		
Tashkent	911,000	Kazakh
Samarkand	195,000	Uzbek
Aral-Balkhash Deserts		
Alma Ata	455,000	Kazakh
Karaganda	398,000	Kazakh
Ashkhabad	170,000	Turkmenian

continued

SIBERIA

West Siberian Agricultural Region		
Novosibirsk	887,000	Russian
Omsk	579,000	Russian
Krasnoyarsk	409,000	Russian
Barnaul	320,000	Russian
Tomsk	249,000	Russian
Altai-Sayan Mountains		
Novo Kuznetsk	377,000	Russian
Prokopyevsk	282,000	Russian
Kemerovo	277,000	Russian
Ob Taiga		
Yenisei Taiga		
Arctic Fringe		
Norilsk	108,000	Russian
Baikalia		
Irkutsk	365,000	Russian
Ulan Ude	174,000	Russian
Chita	171,000	Russian
Lena Taiga		
Yakutsk	74,000	Russian
Northeastern Mountains		
Petropavlovsk	86,000	Russian
Far East		
Khabarovsk	332,000	Russian
Vladivostok	283,000	Russian
Komsomolsk	177,000	Russian

CLIMATIC DATA*

	N. Latitude, degrees	Frost-free days	Average Temperature F. Warmest month	Coldest month	Precipitation, inches
Arkhangelsk	65°	120	60	8	18
Baku	40°	296	79	39	8
Batumi	42°	308	73	44	97
Chelyabinsk	55°	124	66	3	14
Fergana	40°	216	81	27	7
Gorki	56°	149	67	10	23
Irkutsk	52°	95	63	—6	16
Kazan	56°	146	68	8	18
Kharkov	50°	151	69	18	20
Kiev	50°	172	67	21	23
Krasnoyarsk	56°	120	67	—1	12
Leningrad	60°	160	64	18	21
Moscow	56°	130	64	13	24
Omsk	55°	121	66	—3	12
Saratov	52°	161	70	10	15
Tashkent	41°	206	80	30	14
Tomsk	57°	114	64	—3	22
Volgagrad	49°	177	77	14	15
Yalta	45°	245	76	39	22

* Volin, Lazar, *A Survey of Russian Agriculture*, p. 6 .

SOVIET ENERGY RESOURCES*

(in terms of standard fuel units, 7,000 kilocalories per kilogram)

	Production (millions of metric tons)		Reserves (billions of metric tons)
	1958	1965 Plan	1957–59
Coal	365.2	439.2	6,900†
Petroleum	161.9	343.2	5.6
Natural Gas	33.7	177.9	1.8
Peat	20.0	27.	60
Wood for Fuel	24.9	25.7	?
Combustible Shale	4.5	7.5	17
Hydroelectricity	18.2	29.5	?‡
Total	628.4	1,050.0	6,984.4

* U.S. Congress, Joint Congressional Committee on Atomic Energy, *Background Material for the Review of International Atomic Policies and Programs of the United States*, IV, pp. 1647, 1649. Washington, D.C. (Oct. 1960).

† Geological reserves of coal, in billions of tons of natural units, include proven —240, probable—940, and possible—7,500.

‡ Economic potential of hydroelectricity, 1,200 billion kilowatt-hours.

Coal Statistics by Areas*

Reserves in billions of metric tons (000,000,000 omitted)
Production in thousands of metric tons (000 omitted)

Basin	Reserves Total	Valid	Production 1955
Soviet Europe	647.3	74.9	
Pechora	344.5	4.1	14,153
Donets	240.6	57.2	135,334
Kama	30.3	—	—
Moscow	24.3	8.9	39,302
Caucasus	2.0	0.6	2,706
Urals	7.5	5.0	46,857
Western and Eastern Siberia	2,290.0	114.5	—
Kansk-Achinsk	1,220.0	35.0	5,000
Kuznetsk	905.3	70.9	56,537
Irkutsk	88.9	5.2	—
Minusinsk	36.9	2.3	—
Eastern Siberia	5,237.9	4.1	23,173
Lena Basin	2,647.2	1.8	231
Tungus	1,744.8	1.4	2,000
Taimyr	583.5	0.3	—
Ust Yenisei	221.8	—	—
South Yakutsk	40.0	0.7	—
North East	240.0	0.9	—
Transbaikal, Far East, Sakhalin	64.1	8.7	16,057
Bureya	25.0	1.1	—
Sakhalin	20.0	2.1	3,623
Kazakhstan	139.9	29.0	—
Karaganda	51.2	10.3	26,812
Middle Asia	40.8	3.6	6,333
All U.S.S.R.	8,669.5	241.2	376,499

* Hodgkins, Jordan A., *Soviet Power, Energy Resources, Production, and Potentials*, pp. 158–162. New York: Prentice Hall (1960).

Hydroelectric Developments*

† in construction   ‡ proposed

River and Site	Head, in Meters	Capacity, in kilowatts	Completion Date
Volga River: (9 dams)	138	8,300,000‡	
Ivankovo Dam	11	30,000	1937
Uglich Dam	11	200,000	1941
Rybinsk Dam	18	330,000	1941
Gorky Dam	16	400,000	1956
Cheboksary Dam	18	1,000,000‡	
Kuibyshev Dam	23	2,300,000	1957
Saratov Dam	14	1,000,000†	
Volgagrad Dam	22	2,530,000	1961
Astrakhan Dam	5	500,000‡	
Kama River: (4 dams)			
Verkhne Kama Dam	22	400,000‡	
Kama Dam (Perm)	18	504,000	
Votkinsk Dam	17	1,000,000†	
Nizhne Kama Dam	18	1,400,000‡	
Don River			
Tsimlyanskaya Dam	23	164,000	1952
Dnieper River: (14 dams)	100	3,300,000‡	
Kiev Dam	13	200,000‡	
Kanev Dam	11	185,000‡	
Kremenchug Dam	17	624,000†	
Dneprodzerzhinsk Dam	12	350,000†	(1,400,000)
Dnieproges Dam (Zaporozhe)	39	650,000	1932–47
Kakhovka Dam	16	312,000	1956
Svir River: Lakes Onega—			
Ladoga: (2 dams)			
Svir Plant #2		200,000	1952
Svir Plant #3		120,000	1932
Murmansk Area		295,000‡	
Baltic Area		220,000‡	
Lake Sevan—Razdan River:			
Caucasus (9 dams)	1,000	640,000‡	
Sevan Plant	65	32,000	1949
Atarbekyan Dam	135	84,000	1959
Gyumush Dam	300	224,000	1953
Arzni Dam	115	63,000	1956
Kanaker Dam	174	110,000	1937
Yerevan	85	45,000	
Khrami River: Georgia:	876		
(6 dams)	420	723,000‡	
Khrami Dam #1	330	112,800	1949
Khrami Dam #2		250,000	
Khrami Dam #3	550	140,000‡	1961

continued

Urals Area		1,245,000‡	
Central Asia		1,270,000‡	
Ob River: (10 dams)	165	11,850,000‡	
Kamen Dam	54		
Novosibirsk Dam	14	400,000	1957
Baturinsko Dam			
Nizhne Ob Dam	60	6,000,000‡	
Irtysh River: (10 dams)	345	4,500,000	
Bukhtarma Dam	65	540,000	1960
Ust Kamenogorsk Dam	40	450,000	1953
Shulba Dam		1,000,000	
Yenisei River: (6 dams)	52	19,200,000‡	
Sayan Dam	1,600	4,000,000	
Krasnoyarsk Dam	130	5,000,000†	
Yenisei Dam	101	6,000,000‡	
Osinovo Dam		2,000,000‡	
Angara River: (6 dams)	319	14,000,000‡	
Irkutsk Dam	30	660,000	1958
Sukhovo Dam	13	500,000‡	
Telma Dam	12	4,500,000‡	
Bratsk Dam	102		
Ust Ilim Dam	93	3,000,000‡	
Baguchony Dam	69	2,700,000‡	
Amur River: (6 dams)		6,000,000‡	
Zeya River Dam		800,000‡	
Total U.S.S.R.: 120 hydro plants		10,500,000	1958
		23,000,000‡	1965
220 thermal electric plants		42,000,000	1958
		90,000,000	1965
Total U.S.A.: hydro plants		30,098,000	1959
		97,000,000‡	
thermal electric plants		130,121,000	1959

Electric energy per capita per annum
U.S.S.R.   1,115 million kilowatt hours [1959]
U.S.A.   4,159 million kilowatt hours [1959]

* U.S. Congress, Senate Committee on Interior and Insular Affairs and Public Works, *Relative Water and Power Resource Developments in the U.S.S.R. and the U.S.A.* Washington, D.C. (Jan. 4, 1960); and other sources.

SOVIET AND AMERICAN HYDROELECTRIC PLANTS

Name	River	Capacity (Kilowatts)
Krasnoyarsk	Yenisei	5,000,000
Bratsk	Angara	4,500,000
Volgagrad	Volga	2,530,000
Kuibyshev	Volga	2,300,000
Robert Moses	Niagara	2,190,000
	(including Canada	4,560,000)
Grand Coulee	Columbia	1,974,000
Barnhart Island	St. Lawrence	1,824,000
	(U.S. share	900,000)
John Day	Columbia	1,080,000
Hoover	Colorado	1,250,000
Saratov	Volga	1,000,000
Chief Joseph	Columbia	1,028,000
McNary	Columbia	986,000
The Dalles	Columbia	969,000

IRON ORE STATISTICS BY AREAS*

(metric tons, 000,000 omitted)

Area	Production 1955	Production 1965 Plan	Reserves 1956 Tonnage	Reserves 1956 Content
WEST				
Tula & Lipetsk	1.53	1.62	102.2	41.5%
Kursk				
rich ore	—	2.16	634.0	54%
quartzite	0.25	3.71	2,227.8	33%
Krivoi Rog				
rich ore	36.81	49.21	1,592.5	57.3%
quartzite	0.37	14.39	6,548.5	38.0%
Kerch	2.77	9.40	1,658.3	37.2%
Total in West	42.96	87.14	13,745.3	—
EAST				
Magnitogorsk	12.19	9.54	300.1	50.5%
Bakal Region	4.03	5.36	208.5	37.9%
Kachkanarsk	—	4.96	3,900	16.7%
Kustanai				
magnetite	0.24	12.31	1,536.9	46.5%
bog ore	—	2.38	3,368.9	36.8%
Total in East	28.91	70.63	13,338.3	—
SOVIET TOTAL	71.87	158.77	27,083.6	—

* American Iron & Steel Institute, *Steel in the Soviet Union*. New York (1959), pp. 28, 29.

World Reserves of Coal, Petroleum and Natural Gas*

	Coal (billions of short tons)	Petroleum (billions of barrels)		Natural Gas (trillions of cubic feet)	
	Proved	Proved	Potential	Proved	Potential
United States	250	38.2	240	260	1,000
Western Europe	180	1.6	18	5	50
Middle East	?	182.	560	230	2,000
U.S.S.R. and Satellites	270	31.0	120	53	700
China	100	?	?	?	?
World	946	299	1,358	639	4,800

* U.S. Congress, Joint Congressional Committee on Atomic Energy, *Background Material for the Review of the International Atomic Policies and Programs of the United States,* IV, p. 1458. Washington, D.C. (Oct. 1960).

World Consumption of Coal, Petroleum, and Natural Gas*

	Coal (short tons)			Petroleum (million barrels)			Natural Gas (billion cubic feet)		
	1960	1975	2000	1960	1975	2000	1960	1975	2000
United States	450	560	1,000	3,700	6,700	14,000	12,400	26,000	52,000
Western Europe	560	580	600	1,100	2,200	6,000	1,400	3,500	9,000
U.S.S.R. and Satellites	715	1,000	1,130	1,100	3,700	7,400	1,700	15,000	36,000
China	355	920	1,000	28	350	1,000	?	?	?
World	2,319	3,328	4,068	7,284	16,280	38,400	16,370	45,250	104,600

* U.S. Congress, Joint Congressional Committee on Atomic Energy, *Background Material for the Review of the International Atomic Policies and Programs of the United States,* IV, p. 1457. Washington, D.C. (Oct. 1960).

PRODUCTION DATA*

Commodity	1913	1940	1960		1965 Plan
National Income (arbitrary units)	1		22	(1958)	36
Industrial Production (arbitrary units)	1		36	(1958)	66
Coal (million metric tons)	29.2	165.9	513		600/612
Oil (million metric tons)	8.3		148		230/240
Electricity (billion kilowatt hours)	1.9	48.3	292		500/520
Pig Iron (million metric tons)	4.2	14.9	46.8		65/70
Steel (million metric tons)	4.3	18.3	65.3		86/91
Copper (million metric tons)	31	161	416.5	(1959)	772
Cement (million metric tons)			45.5		75/81
Mineral Fertilizers (million metric tons)	69	3,027	13,800		
Grain (billion poods) 1 pood = 36.1 pounds			8.1		10/11
Sugar (thousand metric tons)	1,347		6,400		9,250/10,000 1,800/1,850
Rail transport (billions of ton kilometers)	65.7		1,500		

*Official Soviet data.

Natural Gas Reserves and Production by Areas*

Reserves in billions of cubic meters (000,000,000 omitted)
Production in millions of cubic meters, 1955 (000,000 omitted)

Basin	Reserves	Production
Ukraine	2.5	2,928
North Caucasus	1.5	595
Azerbaidzhan	1.5	1,494
Volga-Ural	2	2,427
Komi A.S.S.R.	1.2	—
Bukhara-Kivin	1.3	—
	10.0	8,981

* Official Soviet data.

Oil Reserves and Production by Areas*

Reserves in millions of metric tons, 1955 (000,000 omitted)
Production in thousands of metric tons, 1955 (000 omitted)

Basin	Reserves	Production	
Ural-Volga	7,424	41,218	(80,000 in 1958)
Azerbaidzhan	994	15,305	
North Caucasus	383	6,524	
Georgia	3	43	
Ukraine	6	531	
Komi-Ukhta	13	553	
Sakhalin	40	950	
Kazakh-Emba	110	1,397	
Turkmen S.S.R.	200	3,126	
Uzbek S.S.R.	20	996	
Kirgiz S.S.R.	5	115	
Tadzhik S.S.R.	2	17	
Total USSR	9,200	70,793	(113,000 in 1958)

Note: One metric ton equals about 7.5 barrels.

*Official Soviet data.

SELECTED READINGS

General Geography

Balzak, S. S., Vasyutin, V. F., and Feigin, Y. G. *Economic Geography of the U.S.S.R.* Translated by Robert M. Hankin and Olga Adler Tittelbaum, edited by Chauncey D. Harris. New York: Macmillan (1949).

Baransky, N. N. *Economic Geography of the U.S.S.R.* Moscow: Foreign Languages Publishing House (1956).

Berg, L. S.: *Natural Regions of the U.S.S.R.* Translated by Olga Adler Tittelbaum, edited by John A. Morrison and C. C. Nikiforoff. New York: Macmillan (1950).

Cole, J. P., and German, F. C., *A Geography of the U.S.S.R.* Washington: Butterworth (1961).

Cressey, George B. *The Basis of Soviet Strength.* New York: Whittlesey House (1945). Translated into Dutch as: *Rusland's Rijkdom.* Utrecht: Kemink.

——. *How Strong Is Russia?* Syracuse: Syracuse University Press (1954).

——. *Asia's Lands and Peoples.* New York: McGraw-Hill, Second Ed. (1951).

Fitzsimmons, Thomas, editor. *Russian Soviet Federated Soviet Republic.* 2 Vols. New Haven: Human Relations Area Files (1957).

——. *U.S.S.R.* New Haven: Human Relations Area Files (1960).

George, Pierre. *U.S.S.R., Haute-Asie–Iran.* Paris: Presses Universitaires de France (1947).

Gray, G. D. B. *Soviet Land.* London: Black (1947).

Gregory, James and Shave, D. W. *The U.S.S.R.* London: Harrap (1944). New York: John Wiley.

Jorré, Georges. *The Soviet Union, the Land and its People.* Translated from French and revised by E. D. Laborde. London: Longmans, Second Ed. (1961).

Leimbach, Werner. *Die Sowjetunion.* Stuttgart: Franck'sche Verlagshandlung (1950).

Library of Congress, *Soviet Geography, a Bibliography.* 2 Vols. Washington (1951).

Mikhailov, Nikolai: *Land of the Soviets.* New York: Furman (1939).

——. *Across the Map of the U.S.S.R.* Moscow: Foreign Languages Publishing House (1960).

——. *Glimpses of the U.S.S.R.* Moscow: Foreign Languages Publishing House (1960).

Shabad, Theodore. *Geography of the U.S.S.R.* New York: Columbia University Press (1951).

——. "Soviet Union", pp. 638–728 in George Hoffman, *A Geography of Europe.* New York: Ronald, Second Ed. (1961).

Specialized Studies

American Steel and Iron Ore Mining Delegation to the Soviet Union. *Steel in the Soviet Union.* New York: American Iron and Steel Institute (1959).

Armstrong, Terence. *The Northern Sea Route.* Cambridge: Cambridge University Press (1952).

Bergson, Abram (editor). *Soviet Economic Growth.* Evanston: Row, Peterson (1953).

Davies, R. A. and Steiger, A. J. *Soviet Asia.* New York: Dial (1942).

Hassmann, Heinrich. *Oil in the Soviet Union.* Princeton: Princeton University Press (1953).

Hodgkins, Jordan A. *Soviet Power, Energy Resources, Production, and Potentials.* Englewood Cliffs: Prentice-Hall (1960).

Hrdlička, Aleš. *The Peoples of the Soviet Union.* Washington: Smithsonian Institution (1942).

Jackson, W. A. Douglas, "The Problem of Soviet Agricultural Regionalization," *Slavic Review*, XX, 656–678 (1961).

Jasay, Naum. *The Socialized Agriculture of the U.S.S.R.* Stanford: Stanford University Press (1949).

Kazakov, George. *Soviet Peat Resources*. New York: Research Program on the U.S.S.R. (1953).

Lamont, Corliss. *The Peoples of the Soviet Union*. New York: Harcourt, Brace (1944).

Lebed, A., and Yakovlev, B. *Soviet Waterways*. München: Institute for the study of the U.S.S.R. (1956).

Mackinder, Halford J. *Democratic Ideals and Reality*. New York: Henry Holt (1942).

Nalivkin, D. V. *The Geology of the U.S.S.R.* Translated by S. I. Tomkeieff, edited by J. E. Richey. New York: Pergamon Press, International series of Monographs on Earth Sciences, VIII (1960).

Saushkin, Julian S., "Economic Geography in the U.S.S.R.," *Economic Geography*, XXXVIII, 28–37 (1962.).

Schwartz, Harry. *Russia's Soviet Economy*. New York: Prentice-Hall (1950).

Shimkin, Demitri B. *Minerals, a Key to Soviet Power*. Cambridge: Harvard University Press (1953).

Suslov, S. P. *Physical Geography of Asiatic Russia (1947)*. Translated by Noah D. Gershevsky, edited by Joseph E. Williams. San Francisco: W. H. Freeman (1961).

Theil, Erich. *The Soviet Far East*. New York: Praeger (1957).

Volin, Lazar. *A Survey of Soviet Russian Agriculture*. Washington: United States Department of Agriculture, Monograph 5 (1951).

Atlases

Atlas C.C.C.P. (Atlas of the U.S.S.R.) Moscow (1955).

Atlas Mira (World Atlas). With English translation volume by Telberg. Moscow (1959).

Atlas Selskago Khoziaistva (Atlas of Soviet Agriculture). Moscow (1961).

Bolshoi Sovietska Atlas Mira (*Great Soviet World Atlas*). With English translation for legends, edited by George B. Cressey. Moscow. Vol. I (1937); Vol. II (1943).

Goodall, George. *Soviet Union in Maps*. London: George Philip; Chicago: Denoyer-Geppert (1954).

Kish, George. *Economic Atlas of the Soviet Union*. Ann Arbor: University of Michigan Press (1960).

Oxford Regional Economic Atlas. *The U.S.S.R. and Eastern Europe*. London: Oxford University Press (1956).

U.S. Central Intelligence Agency. *Atlas of Soviet Administrative Maps*. Washington, D.C. (1960).

Periodicals

Soviet Geography: Review and Translation. New York: American Geographical Society (monthly).

INDEX

(Illustrations are indicated in *italics*.)

THIS BOOK HAS BEEN SET IN 10 POINT LINOTYPE JANSON, LEADED 2 POINTS, PRINTED ON 60 POUND P. H. GLATFELTER ENGLISH FINISH BRITE WHITE SM GRADE PAPER, SIZED FOR OFFSET, AND BOUND IN HOLLISTON ROXITE LINEN OVER 80 POINT BINDERS BOARD.